MAKE · YOUR · OWN

HOW TO CRAFT CANES AND STAFFS FROM RUSTIC TO FANCY

WALKING STICKS

MAKE · YOUR · OWN

How to Craft Canes and Staffs from Rustic to Fancy

WALKING STICKS

by Charles Self

Fox Chapel
PUBLISHING

ACKNOWLEDGMENTS

Special thanks to Bobby Weaver, Sr., for doing the turning for photography, without which this book wouldn't exist, and for providing advice in other areas, without which this book would have been less fun to do. Special thanks also to Gene Bremmer, who supplied diamond willow photos, and to Gilmer Wood Company and Hobbit House Inc., who supplied additional wood photos.

ISBN 978-1-56523-320-1

Publisher's Cataloging-in-Publication Data

Self, Charles R.

    Make your own walking sticks : how to craft canes and staffs from rustic to fancy / by Charles Self. -- East Petersburg, PA : Fox Chapel Publishing, c2007.

    p. ; cm.

    ISBN 978-1-56523-320-1

    Includes index.
    1. Staffs (Sticks, canes, etc.) 2. Staffs (Sticks, canes, etc.)-- Patterns. 3. Wood-carving--Technique. 4. Wood-carving--Patterns. I. Title.

TT199.7 .S45 2007
736/.4--dc22   0706

To learn more about other great books from Fox Chapel Publishing, or to find a retailer near you, call toll-free 800-457-9112 or visit us at *www.FoxChapelPublishing.com.*

Printed in Indonesia
First printing: 2007
Second printing: 2008
Third printing: 2011

Note to Authors: We are always looking for talented authors to write new books in our area of woodworking, design, and related crafts. Please send a brief letter describing your idea to Acquisition Editor, 1970 Broad Street, East Petersburg, PA 17520.

ABOUT THE AUTHOR

Woodworker Charles Self is an award-winning writer who has contributed a vast amount of work to the woodworking field. In 2005, he received a Vaughan-Bushnell Golden Hammer Award for Best Do-It-Yourself Book for *Woodworker's Pocket Reference*. His other books include *Cabinets and Countertops*, *Woodworker's Guide To Selecting & Milling Wood*, *Creating Your Own Woodworking Shop*, and *Building Your Own Home*. He has also written thousands of articles for publications, such as *Popular Woodworking*, *Woodcarving Illustrated*, *Woodshop News*, and *Woodworker's Journal*, and he has edited and consulted for companies such as DeWalt, Grizzly Industrial, McGraw-Hill, Time-Life, and Popular Mechanics Encyclopedia. He currently serves as a director for the National Association of Home & Workshop Writers.

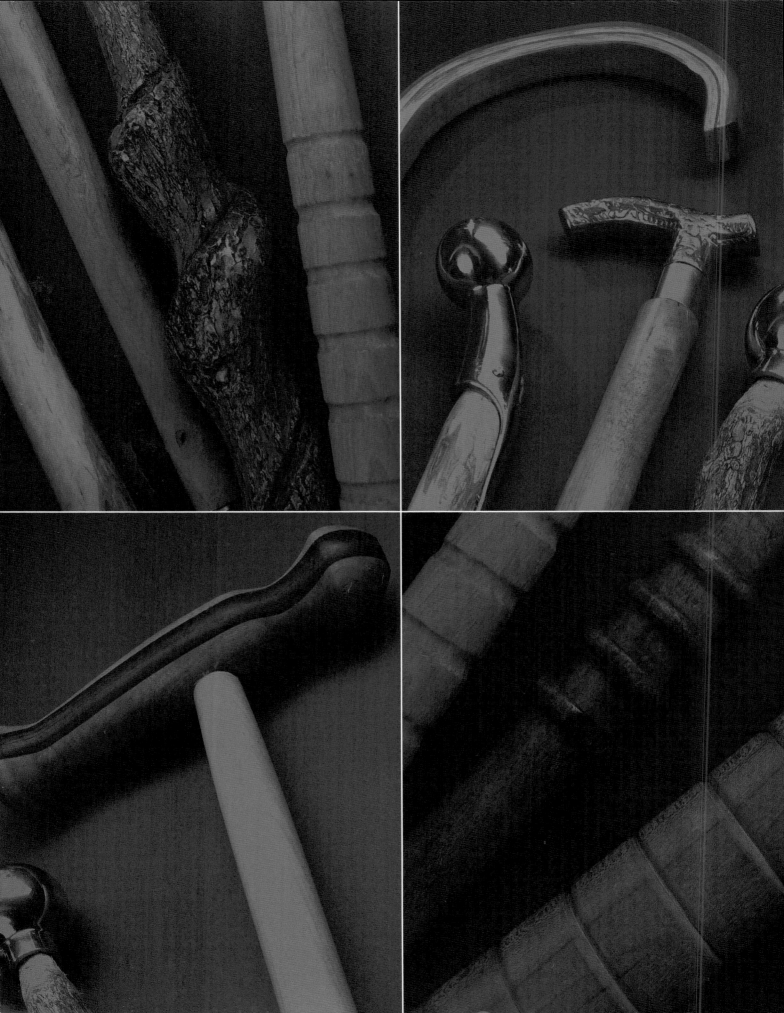

CONTENTS

Introduction:
A Few Good Sticks

These interesting canes are among the projects you will find in this book. You can make most of them with basic shop tools.

Walking sticks, canes, and staffs have been valuable items for a great many centuries, probably ever since someone crawled out of a cave, discovered his leg hurt, and found a branch to add support on that side. Those early walking staffs served much the same purposes they serve today: being useful for those with a sore leg, foot, or hip; handy for drawing maps on the ground; and helpful for pointing out directions.

Once upon a time, gentlemen carried canes as a status symbol, though that use died out many years ago. My own first memory of walking canes is of a shiny black cane given to me by a dapper uncle, about the time that uncle retired from dapperness.

My next memory of small sticks, outside of batons in the hands of orchestra conductors, is from the military. At Parris Island, South Carolina, the Marine Corps drill instructors carried swagger sticks, at least while I was there. They were used more for intimidation than anything else—I don't know of anyone in my generation (or later generations) of Marines who got more than a light tap with the swagger stick. That light tap was more than enough to command attention.

THE POLITICS OF CANES

Over the millennia, walking sticks became important as indicators of power (scepters) and of justice. By the early seventeenth century, because of the use of cane (malacca) as a material for certain types of walking sticks, walking sticks in general began to be known as "canes." For 300 years, the cane was an accessory that denoted wealth when made of expensive or hard-to-work materials. U.S. history shows that Ben Franklin used a gold-headed cane. President Andrew Jackson was the owner of a sword cane, but, given modern times, that's not an item we'll present as a project here.

Use as an offensive weapon, even without a sword, was not unusual. Representative Preston Brooks of South Carolina nearly killed Senator Charles Sumner of Massachusetts in 1856 by beating him with a cane after Sumner insulted a kinsman of Brooks. Back in 1798, Roger Griswold, a Federalist representative, walked across the chamber to Matthew Lyon and pounded on that Republican's head and shoulders with a hickory cane. A few days earlier, Lyon had spit in Griswold's face when Griswold called him a coward, so few were surprised by the caning. Though walking sticks and canes are neither as prevalent nor as in fashion as they once were, they still have a place in modern times.

HANDMADE OR STORE BOUGHT

Walking staffs, or hiking staffs, have gained popularity in recent years as more and more people take to the trails for exercise and fun. They have become much less a statement and much more a utility device for those of us who need a bit of assistance in hobbling along. I doubt my interest in the subject would have reached the stage of construction if I hadn't damaged my knees as a youngster, but, with that damage, I had to take a long look at what the medical suppliers were offering. Adjustable metal canes that feel flimsy and look cheesy just don't do the job.

Store-bought walking staffs are interesting, but they still lack any real variety, mostly being made of aluminum with rubber grips and only the maker's brand for decoration. For woodworkers, that is just not good enough. Making your own walking stick means you'll have the perfect fit and something that makes a statement about who you are. A handmade staff will stand up to rigorous use over time as you use it to balance as you cross a stream on rocks or a log, to judge the depth of the stream if you have to ford it, to check the other side of a large log or rock so you don't step into a nest of snakes, or just to aid you in getting around town.

STICK, CANE, OR STAFF

Let's also take a moment here to talk about what defines a walking stick, a cane, and a staff. Canes tend to have arched tops and to be a bit lower than belt height, possibly 31" to 36". Walking sticks are fairly slender, lack a curved top, and are about the same length as a cane. Walking staffs are breast height or taller in most uses, though they can vary from as short as 40" on up past 54". None of these sizes are set in stone, however, nor are they published as law.

STICK, CANE, AND STAFF FEATURES

Until recently, walking sticks, canes, and staffs have mostly been made out of wood, often mahogany with some ebony, hickory, oak, maple, and other species, too. Today, commercially available ones tend to be made of metal, usually aluminum tubing painted or anodized, and adjustable for height.

As I mentioned earlier, cane handles use a rounded hook, which makes a good handgrip. It is probably related to the old shepherd's crook, with its long shaft and the ending hook that allowed the shepherd to pull a single lamb from the flock. There are also flatter cane handles, as you'll see with a couple of the brass versions, though they do have a slight arc to them.

These curved canes can be made by slicing the wood into thin layers and gluing it together around a form, as you will see later in this book, or by steaming the wood until it softens enough to bend. Steaming is an interesting process, but it is beyond the scope of this book, so we won't cover it here. You can find a little more information in "A Note on Steam Bending" on page 24.

Decorative knobs and handles abound for sticks, canes, and staffs. The most complexly decorated provide a standard cane handle on a tapered cane body, but there are also old hame balls (harness gear for horses) that mount nicely on cane or walking staff bodies.

HOW TO USE THIS BOOK

Within the first section of this book, you'll find everything you'll need to know about getting started making canes: a description of suitable woods and what they're like to work; an introduction to some useful hardware bits and pieces, including handles, joins, and such; a look at some useful tools, both hand and power, for making canes; and some information on finishing. There's also an inspirational gallery from Albert LeCoff, founder of the Wood Turning Center in Philadelphia.

After that, it's on to the projects in the second section of the book. I've included 15 to get you started, ordered from easiest to most complex. The first projects are super-simple variations on a single design, and they're easy to complete, so, even if you've never made a walking stick, cane, or staff before, you should feel at ease making these projects. The first projects also showcase some great ways to modify the designs included here—altering the type of wood suggested, adding a different handle, or using different types of finish. Those looking to further embellish their walking sticks, canes, and staffs will find over 25 original carving patterns from renowned artist Lora S. Irish. Once you've worked through your favorites, you'll be well on your way to making your own designs for a variety of projects.

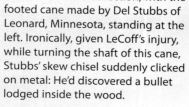

Here's the whole collection, with the footed cane made by Del Stubbs of Leonard, Minnesota, standing at the left. Ironically, given LeCoff's injury, while turning the shaft of this cane, Stubbs' skew chisel suddenly clicked on metal: He'd discovered a bullet lodged inside the wood.

Albert LeCoff Tribute Cane Collection, 1989

Artists: Roger Barnes, Ed Bosley, Rod Cronkite, Frank E. Cummings, III, Walter Dexter, Leo Doyle, Dennis Elliott, David Ellsworth, Giles Gilson, Michelle Holzapfel, Todd Hoyer, C.R. "Skip" Johnson, John Jordan, Bonnie Klein, Frank Knox, "R.W." Bob Krauss, Andreas Kutsche, Dan Kvitka, Stephen Loar, Johannes Michelsen, Bruce Mitchell, Michael Mode, Stephen Paulsen, Michael Peterson, Richard Raffan, Bob Sonday, Ric Stang, Bob Stocksdale, Del Stubbs, Christopher Weiland

H 68" x Diam 24"
Various materials
From the Albert and Tina LeCoff Collection
Photography by John Carlano

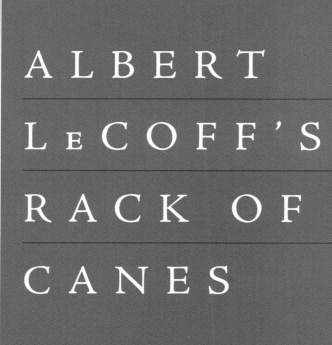

ALBERT LeCOFF'S RACK OF CANES

GALLERY

MANY ARTISTS

The artists and woodturners who made this collection of canes were Roger Barnes, Ed Bosley, Rod Cronkite, Frank E. Cummings III, Walter Dexter, Leo Doyle, Dennis Elliott, David Ellsworth, Giles Gilson, Michelle Holtzapfel, Todd Hoyer, C. R. "Skip" Johnson, John Jordan, Bonnie Klein, Frank Knox, R. W. Bob Krauss, Andreas Kutsche, Dan Kvitka, Stephen Loar, Johannes Michelsen, Bruce Mitchell, Michael Mode, Stephen Paulsen, Michael Peterson, Richard Raffan, Bob Sonday, Ric Stang, Bob Stocksdale, Del Stubbs, and Christopher Weiland. Giles Gilson and Johannes Michelsen made the stand that houses the collection, which you can see if you visit the Wood Turning Center in Philadelphia. The photos were taken by John Carlano.

The magnificent rack of canes on the opposite page belongs to Albert LeCoff, founder of the Wood Turning Center in Philadelphia. The canes were made for his birthday in 1989 by some of the world's leading woodturners to mark LeCoff's many contributions to the field. LeCoff, the victim of a shooting, has a gimpy leg and always walks with a cane, usually one of these fine pieces, which he chooses to suit his mood for the day. He and his wife, Tina, very graciously allowed me to present these canes here. There is a ton of inspiration in these photos of the Albert LeCoff Tribute Cane Collection, and a million ideas to borrow, enhance, and make into your own.

Walter Dexter of Liberty, New York, carved this stalwart eagle atop a turned walnut shaft. Its claw holds a ball at the foot of the cane.

Michelle Holtzapfel of
Marlboro, Vermont,
carved this little creature
as the handle of her cane.

Todd Hoyer of Bisbee, Arizona, found enough mesquite wood attached to this large burl to turn his cane as one piece.

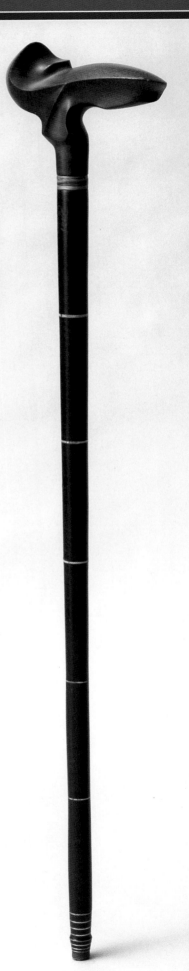

Dan Kvitka of Portland, Oregon, carved this beautiful wenge handle.

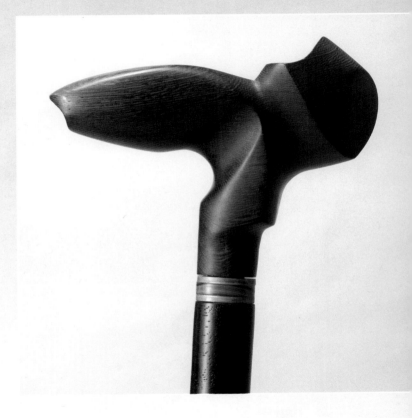

Leo Doyle of San Bernardino, California, created a little gallery of woodturnings at the top of his mahogany cane. He meant the miniatures to represent the many turning exhibitions LeCoff has coordinated.

Johannes Michelsen of Manchester Center, Vermont, built a tiny battery-powered lathe into the handle of his ebony, walnut, and maple cane. The handle conceals not a sword but a miniature turning tool.

David Ellsworth of Doylestown, Pennsylvania, known for virtuoso hollow turning, made this slender cane—actually a lecture pointer—out of a single piece of wood. The ball at the top is turned hollow. He kept the shaft from whipping around by trapping both ends in lathe chucks and applying tension while he turned.

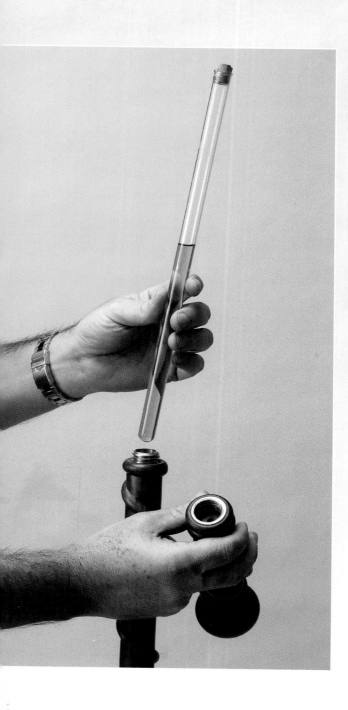

Andreas Kutsche of West Germany turned and carved this cane to resemble a vine-wrapped branch. The top unscrews to reveal a glass vial, which the teetotaler LeCoff fills with . . . tea.

Frank E. Cummings, III of Long Beach, California, turned and carved this elegant cane out of ebony and rosewood, with silver bands and finials.

GETTING STARTED

PART · 1

Before we jump into the walking stick, cane, and staff projects in this book, we'll take a look at some of the different materials, equipment, and techniques you'll want to know for creating these beautiful projects in wood. From choosing and harvesting wood to selecting the right tools and materials to finishing your projects, this section will provide you with all of the information you need to craft not only the projects shown here but also your own versions of sticks, canes, and staffs.

WOODS FOR WALKING STICKS, CANES, AND STAFFS

Selecting the right wood for your walking stick, cane, or staff really comes down to a wood's durability, its availability, and your personal preference. Generally, sticks, canes, and staffs are made of hardwoods for good reason. Hardwood is stronger in almost all ways than most softwood, so it breaks less easily and wears less quickly. Hickory, for example, makes a wonderful cane or walking staff wood, as do maple, locust, and sassafras (which has a wonderful aroma as you're working it). However, almost any wood that turns or scrapes easily is worth considering, even if I don't mention it in this section.

WOOD SPECIES

The list of appropriate woods for walking sticks includes fine hardwoods, such as cherry and walnut, and many of the exotics. More modern examples include mesquite, sassafras, jarrah, and African mahogany (see **Figure 1.1**). The chart on pages 16 to 23 includes photographs of woods to aid you in deciding on appearance. The list is far from complete,

Figure 1.1. Mesquite, here being chamfered with a small plane, is one of the many fine woods you can use for canes. It is hard, lustrous, and takes a beautiful finish.

but it does cover most of the woods of interest to cane makers in this hemisphere. African and Asian woods are available but are not covered here simply because what you see listed is what is most likely to be easily found these days.

A NOTE ON COMBINING WOODS

Woods to be joined must match well: Too much difference in moisture content between two woods creates problems, as do great differences in wood structure. For example, teak, with high silicon and oil contents, does not bond well with any other wood. It is even difficult to bond it to itself, usually requiring an epoxy.

When the same species of wood is used, you get the best gluing results and the longest and strongest hold. For example, attaching pine to pine or walnut to walnut works best. If part is walnut and part is pine, difficulties may arise. However, with small cross sections, as used in most sticks, canes, and staffs, these difficulties aren't going to be overwhelming, provided all the wood is dried to about the same moisture content. None of our projects has extensive wood movement problems because even the larger sticks, canes, and staffs are small as wood projects go.

PLANING FOR CHEAPER WOOD

Saving money by buying rough wood (boards that have not been planed to final size and surface) requires two things: first, patience; second, access to a planer. You'll also need outdoor space where the wood can be stacked with its top covered, so this is not a solution for the city-dwelling woodworker. It is also not a real solution for someone who doesn't have ready access to small sawmills that will sell rough-cut wood. A moisture meter is handy: The model I am currently using has a bottom measure of six percent on a diode light. Six percent is the level recommended for furniture making, but anything under 12% works fine with canes and similar projects.

Planing may take place when moisture levels drop to about 15%. Some hardwoods are difficult to plane on lightweight home shop planers, and wetness doesn't help at all.

Lightweight planers do a fine job of planing many woods, from pine to walnut. They must work harder with white oak, but will do the job if you let them cool down after every 30 minutes of use. These are not production machines. If you treat them like production tools, they'll wear out very quickly.

Cane and stick makers require relatively small amounts of lumber, unless you decide to produce major numbers of gifts or items to sell, so the above advice may not apply to you, but you will be starting a number of projects with wood that is over 1½ inches thick, so seasoning your own wood and smoothing it is a possible money saver.

PURCHASING WOOD

If you're buying these woods from a lumber mill, ask for reasonably straight pieces that are free of checks, cracks, and knots. Finished sizes commonly needed are about 2½" wide by ¾" thick. Reasonably straight and strong woods make the best canes, with the exception of willow or other branches that are twisted from growing with vines curled around them. Properly seasoned wood is easiest to handle, too, and is usually best because you can expect fewer changes (like checks and cracks) from the time it leaves your hands until the time someone uses it.

USING FOUND WOOD

Most wood is readily available at lumber mills or online, but some wood you can gather while walking in the woods (see **Figure 1.2**). Willow shoots come to mind as good finds on a woodsy walk, but if you're not on your own property, it is a very good idea to ask permission before cropping someone else's willow wands, or even sumac and similar bushes. Locating found wood is generally serendipitous—you can sometimes find it in your own backyard, near new contruction sites, and in any number of other places. With a little bit of experience, you'll soon develop an instinct for good sources in your area.

Any of the woods listed in the chart on pages 16 to 23 will work well as found wood or as prepared lumber. Most woods are easy to carve when they're green, but seasoning found wood produces the best and most consistent results. Season found wood slowly to reduce splitting and checking, especially if you've carved patterns in the wood (see the Storing Wood section on page 24 for more information).

Figure 1.2. These pieces of found wood will create fantastic walking sticks and canes.

HARVESTING ROOTS

Roots, which are really just wood that grows below the ground, make interesting canes. If the roots are not large enough for entire sticks, canes, or staffs, they often have shapes that make fantastic handles. Keep an eye open at the base of dead or dying trees, or even at the base of stumps. You may need to clean this wood more thoroughly because it is mostly covered in dirt, but you can otherwise treat it just as you would any other found wood.

If you do much root cutting, a handsaw is quickly ruined. I like a cordless reciprocating saw. Use that with pruning blades either 9" or 12" long and change blades when they're dull. It is heavier than a handsaw, but not too cumbersome to carry.

Sample Swatch	Species	Range	Availability	Cost
	American beech *Fagus grandifolia*	Nova Scotia into Minnesota, south to Florida, eastern Oklahoma, and Texas.	Plentiful.	Moderate.
	American elm *Ulmus americana*	S. Newfoundland, across Canada into the Rockies south through the entire eastern U.S., to Texas.	Generally readily available from dealers in the eastern U.S., but you may be getting one of the other elms instead, because of Dutch elm disease. Most dealers don't differentiate.	Moderate.
	American hornbeam *Carpinus caroliniana*	Most of eastern U.S., into Canada, ranges to Mississippi River, and down to eastern Texas.	Not often available in commercial arenas, but can be found locally.	Cost may be low or high, depending on local availability and demand.
	Andiroba *Carapa guianensis*	Cuba to West Indies, south through Central America, into Brazil, Colombia, Peru.	More plentiful than bigleaf mahogany, grows in pure stands, plentiful enough to be used as a construction timber in areas where it is cut.	Not as available in the U.S. and Europe, but lower in cost than mahoganies.
	Apple *Malus sylvestris*	Worldwide. A cultivar, so planted everywhere desired.	Not commercially available most places (some Piedmont, Virginia, sawmills specialized, at least at times, in apple). Where commercial apple orchards are extensive, it is more available, easier to find. When not found, check firewood piles near apple orchards.	Moderate to high, depending on availability.
	Bigleaf mahogany *Swietenia macrophylla*	S. Mexico to Brazil.	Readily available.	Moderately priced, but rising.
	Black cherry *Prunus serotina*	From Nova Scotia west to Minnesota, south to E. Texas and east to central Florida. Also in west and central Mexico and Guatemala.	Available, reasonably plentiful.	Prices are moderately high and still rising.
	Black locust *Robinia pseudoacacia*	Found in the Appalachian Mts., from Pennsylvania to Alabama and into parts of Arkansas and Missouri. Also naturalized in many other areas in the U.S. and Canada.	Plentiful.	Prices vary with quality and location, but generally moderate to low.
	Black walnut *Juglans nigra*	From Massachusetts to S. Ontario and over to Nebraska, south through the Eastern U.S., except for the coast plain south of Virginia, the gulf coast, and the lower Mississippi valley.	Readily available.	Cost has risen recently, but is still moderate when compared to imports.
	Black willow *Salix nigra*	Most of the Eastern U.S. and into Canada, with none in Florida.	Readily available in the commercial market. This is another wood that is searched out in the shoot stage to be dried for stick making.	Low to moderate.

Appearance and Workability	Notes
Dark to light reddish brown heartwood, little white sapwood. Small, numerous rays. Silvery sheen. Quarter-Sawn lumber very attractive. Hard, heavy, strong, uniform in texture. High in strength and shock resistance. Somewhat difficult to work with hand tools, but works easily with power tools. Bends readily with steam. Fine for walking sticks, canes, staffs.	Not durable. Shrinks a lot during seasoning and is not dimensionally stable when seasoned.
Grayish brown with a reddish tinge. White sapwood. Low to medium luster. Coarse texture and grain, usually with straight grain that can be irregular. Quarter-Sawn surfaces show fine uniform rings. Hard, medium heavy, tough. Excellent bending qualities. Resists abrasion well. Works well, but doesn't polish easily. Careful finishing needed to get rid of sawing fuzz. Dulls tools quickly. Doesn't split well. Takes nails and screws well. Glues up nicely. Takes all usual finishes. Works well for walking sticks, canes, staffs.	Not durable. Needs care during drying to prevent twisting and warping.
Pale yellow to a very pale tan. Dense, smooth, with a subtle figure, abrupt grain changes. Medium weight, strong. Sometimes hard to work, care needed in gluing, planing. Finishes very well, can be finished with a single coat of wax. Great for walking sticks, canes.	Not durable. Difficult to season because it warps easily. Slow drying and careful, weighted stickering are essential.
Reddish brown heartwood, pinkish sapwood. Similar to hard maple or cherry. Turns nicely, finishes very well with few coats of finish. Decent bending qualities. Good walking staff, cane wood.	Moderately difficult to season, high shrinkage, warping may be a problem, but still has greater stability than many tropical hardwoods of greater repute.
Light tan with streaks and wide bands of darker brown. Hard, heavy, close grained, with imperceptible pores and rays. Unusual grain patterns contribute great beauty to work (as well as difficulty in working the wood). Transition from early to latewood is gradual. May be hard to machine. Works easily with proper and extremely sharp tools. Glues and finishes well. Can be readily bent (steam or just heat). Turns well if straight sections are available. Available only in short lengths, seldom consistently. Look for small limbs from own trees or from orchards doing pruning. Good for walking sticks, canes, staffs.	Not durable. Difficult to season to prevent warping and checking. Stable once seasoned.
Varies from light gray-tan to true mahogany red. Moderately coarse texture. Weight varies from light to medium. Strength to weight ratio is good. Hardness may vary from lower than tulip poplar to harder than oak. Cuts well with hand and machine tools. Carves easily and holds edges. Filling is needed to create a glass smooth finish, but it accepts all finishes well. Works well for walking sticks, canes, staffs.	Very durable. Seasons easily with little shrinkage and is stable after seasoning.
Sapwood varies from pale brown-white to pink. Heartwood is a characteristic cherry red-brown. Darkens with age, becoming a richer, deeper red-brown. Rich luster. Straight grain, with frequent wavy streaks. Lovely figure on quarter-sawn cherry. Medium heavy wood, with excellent strength properties. Works very well: saws cleanly, planes neatly, turns beautifully. Good screw holding. Glue adheres well. Takes most finishes exceptionally well. Cherry has been used for centuries for walking sticks, canes, staffs.	Not durable. Seasons easily and well, air or kiln dries with good results, slight tendency to warp that can be corrected by weighting the stock as it dries.
Heartwood varies from greenish yellow to dark or golden brown that turns to deep russet when exposed to the air. Luster is fairly high. Heavy, with straight grain and uneven texture. Stronger and stiffer than white oak. Very good bending properties, comparable to ash and beech. Difficult to work with hand tools, but machines easily. Takes a very smooth finish that will accept a high polish. Not easy to nail. Glues satisfactorily.	Heartwood is exceptionally durable, but sapwood decays readily. It must be seasoned slowly, and even then shows some tendency to warp. Once dried, it is stable.
Heartwood is a rich, purplish brown, or (if immature) warm chocolate brown without the purple overtones. Moderately coarse, uniform texture. Many figure types. Strong, heavy, but light compared to woods of similar strength. Works easily with all tools. Worked edges remain sharp. Excellent for turning, spindle molding, routing, and carving. Little tendency to split with nails or screws. Filling the pores provides a supremely flat surface that takes a velvety luster. Glues well, and the wood stains evenly. Great for walking sticks, canes, staffs.	Needs slow drying, remains exceptionally stable once dried. Heartwood is durable. Steaming during kiln drying creates a slightly muddy brown color, eliminating all the purple overtones.
Heartwood is a pale reddish brown to a gray-brown. Sapwood is a white-tan to a light tan. Grain is interlocked, texture is uniform. One of the lightest domestic hardwoods. Hard to machine because of the interlocked grain. Glues well. Takes a good finish. Good carving wood. Useful for walking sticks, canes, staffs.	Not durable. Tends to warp during seasoning, but has good stability once dried.

Sample Swatch	Species	Range	Availability	Cost
	Blackgum *Nyssa sylvatica*	All eastern states, Maine to Michigan, Illinois, Mississippi, and south to Texas.	Readily available.	Inexpensive.
	Boxelder *Acer negundo*	Quebec west to Alberta, south to Florida.	Usually mixed with other soft maples, abundant.	Low.
	Butternut *Juglans cinerea*	From Quebec south through the NE part of the U.S., west to North Dakota, as far south as Alabama.	Supplies are limited and diminishing. Currently more valued for its nuts than its lumber.	Moderate.
	Chechem *Metopium browneii*	Dom. Republic, Cuba, Jamaica, N. Guatemala, Belize, Mexico to the Yucatan.	The Forest Production Society of Quintana Roo, Mexico, is working to commercialize chechem, and other woods, as substitutes for endangered species. Supplies are irregular.	Mid-range.
	Ebony blackbean (Texas ebony) *Ebenopsis ebano*	S.W. Texas into Mexico and the Yucatan.	Limited growth range, often small size of trees keep supplies low.	Expensive.
	Giant chinkapin *Chrysolepis chrysophylla*	Pacific coast region of U.S. into coastal ranges of central California.	Rare.	Fairly expensive.
	Goncalo alves *Astronium fraxinifolium*	Guyana, Colombia, Ecuador, Mexico, Peru, Guatemala, Honduras, El Salvador, Trinidad, and Brazil.	Limited supply in U.S. Durable and useful wood, so even though it is abundant in its range, little gets exported.	Costly when available.
	Honey mesquite *Prosopis glandulosa*	Mesas, canyons, and desert plains of the more arid regions of California, Nevada, Arizona, New Mexico, Texas, Kansas, and Oklahoma.	Commercially available, but not readily available except by mail order. Limited quantities make it to market.	Moderate.
	Ipe *Tabebuia serratifolia*	Throughout tropical South and Central America and to a smaller extent in the Lesser Antilles.	Widely available.	Moderate.
	Live oak *Quercus virginiana*	On the U.S. coast plain, from SE Virginia through S. Florida and the Keys, to SW Oklahoma and into mountainous NW Mexico.	Not marketed commercially to any extent, but is sometimes available in limited supply.	Moderate.
	Magnolia *Magnolia grandiflora*	Coastal band no more than 100 miles wide from SE North Carolina to Mississippi, SE Louisiana, and into E. Texas.	Not widely distributed, but is available within its growth region.	Moderate.
	Northern red oak *Quercus rubra*	S. Quebec to central Alabama, E. Nebraska to the Atlantic.	Plentiful.	Low.

Appearance and Workability	Notes
Pale brown-gray heartwood, yellow to light brown. No luster. Uniform texture, close interlocked grain. Medium light for a hardwood. Difficult to split and nail. Worked with care, it rewards the effort, as it glues well and finishes very nicely, with smooth, bright surfaces.	Interlocked grain makes it hard to season, twists and warps badly unless carefully handled. Not durable.
Yellowish brown but pale with pale yellow-green sapwood. Some coral-red streaks can be caused by a fungus. The lightest of the American maples. Easily workable with both machine and hand tools.	Not durable, dries well, stable after drying.
Heartwood is light chestnut brown, with darker zones. White sapwood. Satiny, generally straight grain. Light for a hardwood. Lacks stiffness, moderately weak in bending strength, and in compression. Easily worked with sharp edges. Takes a lustrous finish. An excellent carving wood.	Not durable. Dries easily, with minimal shrinkage. Stable when dry.
Deep brown heartwood almost the color of black walnut. Sapwood is yellow-brown. Varies from red, with a slight greenish tint and a golden luster, to plain brown. Very attractive plain cut grain pattern. Very hard, strong, fine and uniform texture. Heavy. Works well with sharp tools. Takes glue readily. Polishes to a fine finish. Similar to hard maple in workability, but a bit stringier. Fine for walking sticks, canes, staffs.	No data on durability, has caustic exudates that make handling the raw (undried) wood unpleasant. Said to be as hard on allergic people as poison oak. This wood might reward further investigation.
Clear yellow sapwood, reddish brown heartwood tinged with purple. Very strong. Very heavy, compact, close grained, and hard. Fine texture, straight grain, outstanding sheen that takes a high natural polish. Works carefully with hand tools. Machines and turns easily. Useful for canes and walking sticks when available.	Durable. Not much information available on seasoning.
Light brown sapwood and nearly identical heartwood. Heavy, hard. Straight grain. Works easily when properly seasoned. Machines, glues, sands, finishes easily. Good for canes, walking sticks.	Not durable, difficult to cure.
Light golden brown to reddish brown heartwood, with dark brown streaks. Irregular grain. Hard, heavy, dense. Difficult to work, depending on density of a particular piece. Turns nicely, finishes with a good shine.	Most is used locally.
Light to dark cocoa or chocolate brown, with narrow yellow-brown sapwood. Fine, wavy grain, frequently interlocked or cross-grained. Excellent luster. Very hard, very heavy, medium to coarse texture. High strength. Brittle. High elasticity. Cross-grain difficult to work. Sands and polishes well. Turns well.	Very durable. Can be air dried without problems.
Wide, yellowish-white sapwood, differentiated from grayish green to brown-olive heartwood. Fine but often uneven and interlocked grain. Very heavy, very hard. Difficult to work, and dulls cutters quickly on machine tools. Turns and finishes well. Works well for walking sticks, canes, staffs.	Extremely durable. Seasons easily, without warping or checking. Stable after seasoning.
Yellow-brown. Very hard and heavy. One of the heaviest U.S. domestic woods. Uneven grain pattern, often contorted. Extremely hard to work. Difficult to turn, but finishes well. Holds nails and glues well (after pre-boring as needed). Works well for walking sticks, canes, staffs if you like a challenge.	Extremely durable. Must be protected from too rapid drying, with protection from direct sun, coated ends of logs, to prevent checking.
Light to dark brown heartwood usually tinged with yellow or green, with occasional green-black or purple-black streaks. Sapwood is yellow-white. Uniform in texture, straight-grained, stiff, hard. High shock resistance. Moderately heavy. Works easily with all tools. Takes a good finish. Nailing and gluing properties are adequate or better. Good for walking sticks, canes, staffs.	Not durable. Seasons easily, without warping, and stays flat.
Light reddish tan heartwood, almost white sapwood. Prominent rays darker in color than those of white oak. Hard and heavy. Porous. More elastic than white oak, but weaker in shear parallel to the grain. Machines reasonably well. Takes finishes well, but needs a filler. Works well for walking sticks, canes, staffs.	Not durable. Above average shrinkage during drying, so pile needs weights to reduce warping.

Sample Swatch	Species	Range	Availability	Cost
	Nutmeg hickory *Carya myristiaeformis*	From north-central Texas to South Carolina.	Not as available as other hickories, but is marketed with the other pecans so that doesn't raise the price. If you want to make sure you're getting nutmeg hickory, you may have to cut your own.	Moderate.
	Osage orange *Maclura pomifera*	SW half of Arkansas to SE Oklahoma, into eastern Texas. Also planted throughout the Mississippi Basin.	Low availability because of tree size, small range, general lack of use.	Seldom available as logs or veneer, but can often be found from independent sawyers in its range.
	Pacific madrone *Arbutus menziesii*	SW British Columbia through Washington, Oregon, and California in coastal mountains.	Not shipped, so hard to find.	Moderate to high, with burls very costly.
	Pear *Pyrus communis*	Throughout Europe, Asia, U.S.	Most supplies from Europe, limited because only old trees are cropped from orchards. Mostly veneer is imported. U.S. supplies are also scarce, and quality is lower than pear from overseas.	Veneer is costly.
	Pecan *Carya illinoinensis*	From Indiana to the SE corner of Wisconsin, Iowa, Kansas and into Alabama, Texas, and Mexico.	Lumber, veneers, and plywood are readily available.	Moderate.
	Persimmon *Diospyros virginiana*	S.E. U.S., except for S. Florida. North to Connecticut and New York, west to Iowa and Kansas, south to Texas.	Not scarce, but hard to find most of the time.	Expensive.
	Pink peroba *Aspidosperma polyneuron*	NE Brazil, Argentina.	Availability is probably better than any other Brazilian hardwood.	Moderate.
	Purpleheart *Peltogyne paniculata*	From Sao Paulo to Trinidad and Panama.	Not widely found in the U.S., but readily available in turning blank and block sizes.	Moderately expensive.
	Red alder *Alnus rubra*	Pacific Cost, Alaska down to central California.	Plentiful.	Low.
	Red maple *Acer rubrum*	Eastern N. America from Florida to Newfoundland, also Texas.	Abundant, sold as generic soft maple.	Low.
	Sassafras *Sassafras albidum*	Coast of S. Maine to S. Ontario, Michigan, Iowa and Kansas, on south to Florida and Texas.	Can be hard to find because it is usually mixed with other woods, particularly ash. If you learn to distinguish them, it will be easier to locate sassafras later. Has a distinctive aroma that is pleasing to most people.	Moderate to low.

Appearance and Workability	Notes
Reddish brown heartwood contrasts sharply with white sapwood. Hard and heavy. Identical in density to sugar maple. Less dense than true pecan. Very strong, elastic. Softest wood in the pecan group, but hard enough to rapidly dull tools. Turns nicely, polishes to a soft glow. Good for canes, walking staffs.	Not durable. Lots of shrinkage from wet to dry, so careful seasoning is needed.
Golden yellow fresh cut heartwood, with some reddish streaks. Turns deep red-brown on exposure to air. Sapwood is thin and white. High luster. The wood is very heavy, hard, tough, and resilient. Difficult to work. Nails only with difficulty, but holds screws well. Glues easily. Oils accelerate the deepening of the color when finishing. Good for walking sticks, canes, staffs when available.	Durable. Seasons well, very stable after seasoning.
Pale salmon. Hard, heavy, and strong. Smooth grain. Glues poorly. Works reasonably well. Polishes up beautifully.	Not durable, hard to season, hard to find anywhere outside the West Coast.
Pinkish brown, heartwood often darker. Straight grained, texture is close and uniform. Heavy. Planes to a silky sheen. Similar strength properties to oak, though tougher to split. Glues easily. Stains and finishes well. Works well with tools in any direction. Sands smooth. Turns well. Carves sweetly. Nail and screw holding properties are good. Would be good for canes if it were easier to find.	Not durable. Air dries slowly, and will distort badly if not heavily weighted. Stable after drying.
Brownish sapwood, brown and reddish brown heartwood. Heavy and strong. Conspicuous rays. Needs careful machining. Planes readily. Turns nicely. Needs extensive sanding. Fine for canes, walking staffs.	Not durable. Seasons easily if kiln dried, not at all easily if air dried.
Black heartwood in a narrow band on older trees. Creamy white sapwood mottled with dark spots that turn gray-brown when exposed to air. Close grained, hard, tough, and strong. Heavy, medium to fine texture, with very little figure. Difficult to work with any tools. Finishes to a high polish. Does not glue well. High shock resistance. Holds nails well. Surface stays smooth even under hard use.	The black heartwood resists decay.
Varies from light brown to pink to red, sometimes with brown, pink, or purple streaks. Works well. Finishes smoothly. Polishes out nicely. Glues well.	In Brazil, entire buildings are made of pink peroba.
Pinkish cinnamon sapwood with light brown streaks. Dull brown heartwood that oxidizes to violet purple and then black. Medium luster. Straight grain, even fine texture. Hard, strong, very heavy. Great shock absorption qualities. Must be worked slowly. Tear out when planing because the grain is interlocked. Glues well. Finishes nicely, and often only wax is applied in order to help maintain the purple color. Stable in use. Fine for walking sticks, canes, staffs.	Very durable. Seasons well and quickly, though there is some difficulty in fully drying the centers of thick planks.
Ranges from white to pinkish to light brown. Fairly soft. Easily worked by sharp tools. Turns decently. Carves well. Glues well. Figure can be stained to mimic cherry.	
Light brown heartwood, sometimes gray, green, or purplish tinge. White sapwood. Turns well. Planes well. Finishes smooth. Easy to work.	Not durable, may stain during drying, check against hard (sugar) maple with ferrous sulfate spotted on—red maple turns dark blue, sugar maple turns green.
Pale brown heartwood deepens to orange-brown on exposure. Narrow yellowish sapwood. Resembles white ash. Soft, brittle, straight coarse grained. Slightly aromatic scent. Medium weight. Coarse texture. Medium luster. Interesting grain pattern. Works easily with all tools. Takes a very nice finish. Nails must be used with care, but screws hold well. Glues well. Stable after drying. At least two of our projects are in sassafras.	Very durable. Very easy to season, though it may check some.

Sample Swatch	Species	Range	Availability	Cost
	Shagbark hickory *Carya ovata*	S. Maine west to Minnesota (SE), south to east Texas, east to Georgia, on into New Hampshire, avoiding the coastal plains of the Carolinas.	Readily available.	Moderate to high.
	Sourwood *Oxydendrum arboreum*	S. Pennsylvania west to Indiana, south to W. Florida and eastern Louisiana.	Sourwood has become an ornamental in some urban areas, which may provide a starting point in the search for this fine wood. It is seldom found as a commercial wood.	Moderate.
	Spanish cedar *Cedrela odorata*	West Indies, Central, S. America, except Chile.	Heavily used in its native range, but still available at specialty lumber dealers.	Reasonable prices.
	Sugar maple *Acer saccharum*	Not in Florida, South Carolina, Delaware, otherwise every state east of Great Plains, eastern Canada.	Abundant, highly figured less available and more costly.	Middle to high.
	Sweet gum *Liquidambar styraciflua*	Florida to Connecticut, west to Illinois, Mississippi, Oklahoma, and Texas.	Heartwood marketed as red gum, often half a tree's volume. Sapwood sold as sapgum. Adequate supplies.	Moderate to low.
	Sycamore *Platanus occidentalis*	Eastern half of U.S., from S. Maine to SE Nebraska, south into Texas and along the Gulf to N. Florida.	Readily available.	Moderate for a domestic hardwood.
	White ash *Fraxinus americana*	From Nova Scotia and Maine west to Minnesota, south to Texas and Florida. All states east of the Mississippi, and as far west as Kansas and Oklahoma.	Plentiful.	Low to moderate.
	White birch *Betula papyrifera*	Throughout Canada, most of Northern U.S. into West Virginia and North Carolina.	Widely available.	Mixed with the other two major birches, yellow and sweet. Moderate.
	White oak *Quercus alba*	S. Quebec, S. Ontario, Minnesota, Nebraska, to Florida and Texas.	Veneers are plentiful, lumber is available widely.	Moderate.
	Yellow birch *Betula alleghaniensis*	From SE Manitoba to NE U.S.	Widely available.	Moderate.
	Yellow poplar *Liriodendron tulipfera*	S. New England to S. Michigan, south to west central Louisiana and N. Florida.	Readily available.	Inexpensive.

Appearance and Workability	Notes
Brown to reddish brown heartwood. Sapwood is most valuable, wide, and nearly white. Hardest, heaviest, strongest North American wood in common use. Coarse texture, straight grain, outstanding elasticity. Works fantastically with sharp tools. Finishes very smoothly. Great for walking sticks, canes, staffs.	Not durable. Needs careful seasoning to prevent checks, splits, warping.
Attractive pinkish brown color, wide sapwood, yellowish brown to a light pink. Heartwood is brown with tinges of red and pink that becomes dull on exposure. Very similar in color to maple. High luster. Heavy. Subdued grain lines. Works well with hand or machine tools. Holds sharp, crisp edges nicely. Glues well. Sands nicely. Finishes very well. Useful for canes and walking sticks.	Not durable. Marked tendency to warp, with high shrinkage rates.
Pinkish to reddish brown hardwood. Color and figure can be confused with bigleaf mahogany. Soft. Light weight. Fine textured. Distinct cedar odor. Works easily. Finishes nicely. Good dimensional stability. Useful for walking sticks, canes, staffs.	Durable, dries rapidly without warping or splitting.
Turns well, works well, finishes well, takes stain well.	May stain during drying. Bends well.
Heartwood is bright brown with red tints. Sapwood (often marketed separately) is creamy white. Ribbon stripes are common. Often marketed as red gum, due to color of heartwood. Interlocked grain. Satin luster. Uniform in texture. Heavy, moderately strong, and stiff. Often available in wide boards. Works very easily with all tools. Planes well, sands to a good surface. Does not tend to split when nailed and holds nails and screws well. Does not steam bend well. Provides beautiful veneer that readily stains to look like cherry, maple, or mahogany. Good for walking sticks, canes, staffs that do not need a bend.	Not durable. Large, fairly fast-growing tree (for a hardwood), diameter to 3', height to 120', so wide boards are often found. Seasons very easily.
Heartwood is various shades of reddish brown. Sapwood can be an almost silvery white. Silver brought out by quarter sawing. Warps and twists incredibly if flat sawn. Quarter sawn preferable. Medium weight. Very firm, tough, and strong. Medium texture. Irregular grain. Interwoven fibers require cautious working. Turns easily. Holds nails and screws well; may split unless pre-bored. Glue works well. Finishes smoothly. Responds well to stains. Works okay for walking sticks, canes, staffs.	Not durable. Keep from ground contact. Seasoning must be done carefully, and milling should emphasize quarter sawing to reduce warping. Very stable after drying if quarter sawn.
Heartwood is brown to dark brown, sometimes with a hint of red. Strong, hard, and heavy. Straight, close grain. Steam bends well. Easy to work. Only dulls tool edges slightly. Does not split easily when nailing. Glues well. Takes most finishes well. Good for walking sticks, canes, staffs.	Not durable. Dries more quickly than other woods. Is stable after seasoning.
Creamy white. Moderately heavy. Uniform texture. Lower shock resistance than yellow birch. Works well. Finishes nicely. Holds nails and screws well.	Not durable. As with other birches, commercial importance and current fashion may drive price.
Light tan to brown heartwood. Narrow, nearly white sapwood. Very attractive. Heavy, strong, hard. Moderately fine grain. Quarter sawing reveals large number of rays. Straight grain. Good steam bending wood. Superb wear (abrasion) resistance. Works fairly easily. Finishes smooth. Glues satisfactorily. Works well for walking sticks, canes, staffs.	Seasons slowly, tends to check and split, but movement once dry is medium or less. Noted for durability: have seen white oak picnic tables that have lasted 20 years. But they're not much fun to move for mowing.
Reddish brown heartwood. Light yellow sapwood. Hard. Often wavy grained. Bends well. Needs care in glue-up. Works nicely with power tools. Takes a good finish.	Not durable. Commercially important in eastern Canada and northeastern U.S., so demand may drive price strongly.
Heartwood is brown to pale yellow, turning greenish when cut. Often has fast-fading magenta mineral inclusions. Lightweight. Fine texture. Straight grained. Weak, somewhat brittle, only moderately strong. Taste and odor free. Works easily with all tools. Nails and screws easily, but doesn't hold nails well. Not often used under clear finishes because of its greenish cast. Takes paint well. Carves very well. Turns nicely. Can often be found in wide boards. Useful for canes, sticks.	Not durable. Seasons easily, is stable after drying.

STORING WOOD

Despite your best plans, you may not be able to make your cane or staff as soon as you buy or find the wood. If you store the wood properly, it will be available for you when you're ready and not have lost any of its quality.

To properly store prepared wood, simply stack it horizontally with supports every 12" until the moisture content is at an appropriate level (under 12 percent) (see **Figure 1.3**). A moisture meter is handy for this process, giving you the exact moisture percentage for the wood. Otherwise, dry any wood about a year for each inch of thickness.

Photo courtesy of Hardwood Information Center

Figure 1.3. Properly stored prepared wood is stacked horizontally with supports and stickers to achieve a 12 percent or lower moisture percentage. Though this is, of course, more wood than most woodworkers have on hand, it is still an excellent example of how to properly store wood.

To properly store found wood, like willow wands or vine-twisted sassafras, first remove any dirt, dust, or other debris using a rag and water. You can also use a drawknife to clean the bark off, if desired. Then, stack it horizontally with supports every 12" and wait until it reaches the appropriate moisture content, just as you would with prepared wood.

BENDING WOOD

Most North American woods, hard or soft, bend decently, but not all do. Many fruitwoods, like apple, might bend well if found in longer lengths without many knots, but, because most fruitwood branches come from orchards, finding bendable lengths of 40" is not easy. Red cedar is also a problem because it often has lots of knots that tend to snap when the wood is bent. Red and white oak, ash, sweet gum, alder, hickory, maple, black locust, tulip poplar, magnolia, and similar woods all bend well in thin strips, as do walnut and cherry, our premier furniture woods. Some exotics don't bend well at all, even in thin strips.

A NOTE ON STEAM BENDING

In this book, I've chosen to use lamination, rather than steam bending, for the sticks and canes with curved handles because lamination is easier and requires less gear. However, steam bending is a reasonably simple process and thus a practical alternative to lamination. Both processes allow you to create rounded edges and other effects for your finished projects.

If you decide to try steam bending, realize that you must find a source of steam and create a place to catch the steam. (Be sure that you do not use PVC plumbing pipe in this process, because it bends when it gets hot and makes a mess.) Lee Valley offers a group of products, including an instruction manual, that can be a big help in steam-bending work.

SIZING WALKING STICKS AND CANES

Before you select the wood for your project, it's important to know what you want the finished size to be. When you make your own cane or stick, you can readily, and easily, adjust it for height. A walking stick might be as little as 42 inches long or on up past 54 inches, if desired. To size a single-purpose walking stick, hold out your hand at a comfortable angle, imagine you have a stick in your hand and are walking on rough ground. Measure, or get someone to measure, from that hand to the ground, and you'll have a near perfect fit (see **Figure 1.4**). Try it with a branch or a narrow ripping to be sure.

With a knob handle, the walking stick may become a cane, providing walking support even on smooth surfaces for those with leg problems. Canes are shorter than walking sticks and should be measured so that the arm is slightly bent at the elbow and the wrist, with the hand falling naturally. Drop a tape to the ground from the curled palm of the hand. Confirm the measurement by experimenting with a cane blank sawn out of pine. Make it longer than you think it ought to be, and then shorten it an inch at a time.

Total cane length depends on user height. For general use, 34 inches works for moderately tall people, while 30 inches works for fairly short people. As with all canes, measurements are approximate and need to be fitted to the wood on hand, the fittings on hand, and the user's needs as far as size and appearance go. Measurement of overall height must always allow for a couple of inches of

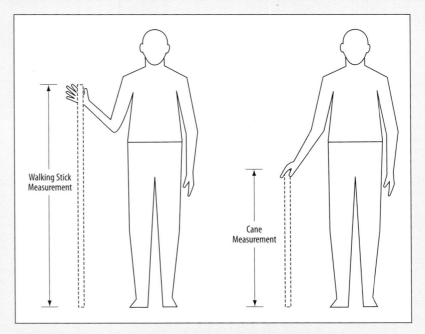

Figure 1.4. To figure out the proper length of your walking stick or cane, imagine you have the stick in your hand and are walking with it; then, drop a measuring tape to the ground from your hand.

rise for the handle, about half an inch rise for the brass joint, if any, and almost no rise for a rubber tip. Be sure to figure in this extra rise.

Size handles to fit a particular hand, unless you're using a naturally shaped limb or root; then, nature determines the sizing. Even with a natural handle, it's best to use smaller crooks or roots for people with smaller hands. Handle size is not an imperative for most people, but it does add to comfort. Take a rough measurement of the lightly closed hand across the palm side to get the thumb knuckle in. If the result is 4", add an inch or an inch and a half and use that for a handle length. Handles about an inch in diameter seem to be nearly universal, though some are slightly thinner or thicker.

ADHESIVES, HARDWARE, AND FASTENERS

Producing sticks and canes successfully, whether a single project or a dozen different projects (or one project a dozen different times) means applying an appropriate adhesive, using correct clamping, allowing plenty of drying time, and choosing and using the right hardware and fasteners. We'll look at the materials involved with those steps in this section.

There's not a lot of hardware that goes into making walking sticks, canes, and staffs—not even such project standbys as hinges and nails. But there are several specialty pieces that are helpful, and a couple that are close to essential unless you're making a natural shape from willow or sumac—and even there, a tip of rubber or metal is handy.

ADHESIVES

The basic needs for wood glues when building sticks, canes, and staffs are good strength and high water resistance or waterproofing. My personal recommendation is to go with Titebond II for all stick and cane construction that needs glue; use epoxy for adding decorative touches. Otherwise, almost any other wood adhesive is cheaper than epoxy, easier to work with, and just as strong as you need. But let's take a closer look so you can make choices according to the qualities of your particular cane.

For general uses, liquid yellow glues and polyvinyl acetate (white resin) glues are best. The yellow glues include the water-resistant Titebond II and the waterproof Titebond III, which I prefer to epoxy when epoxy's other special qualities—gap filling, adhesion to oily woods, joining dissimilar materials—aren't needed.

For waterproofing beyond that offered by yellow glues or polyvinyl acetate, choose epoxy or polyurethane—select polyurethane first unless the epoxies fill some other specific need. Epoxies are too costly for general use.

Resorcinol is another type of waterproof glue that is less often used today. It is a two-part glue, with one part a powdered catalyst and the other a liquid. It has been used in boatbuilding for decades and is available around waterfronts as well as online. At 70°F, it has a working time of 15 minutes; the time shortens as the shop temperature increases. Like epoxy, resorcinol emits a noxious vapor and must be used in a well-ventilated area with the user's body surfaces, particularly the eyes, protected. New safety glasses provide high and low protection and wrap around very well on the sides.

Let's look at these specific types of glue—aliphatic resins, polyurethanes, and epoxies—so that you understand the advantages and disadvantages of each.

ALIPHATIC RESIN GLUE

Inexpensive, water-resistant glues, like aliphatic resin glues, are superb for the sticks and canes builder (see **Figure 1.5**). In my experience, Titebond II wood glue is a heat-resistant, waterproof, liquid polyaliphatic resin glue that is sufficiently waterproof to be used everywhere but below water lines. It is similar in joint appearance to other yellow glues but sets even more rapidly. (Chemists have provided Titebond II Extend for those of us who don't move very quickly during assembly.) Initial tack is strong, set is fast (about five minutes), and gumming is minimal during sanding. Clamp for about one half hour. All Titebond glues are a bit more sensitive to temperature, at least on the cold side, than regular aliphatic resin glues: I used Titebond II for some winter projects and got chalky glue when shop temperatures were below about 60°F.

Titebond II and Titebond III are modestly more expensive than standard Titebond. Such waterproof and highly water-resistant glues are not really for everyday use, though a lot of woodworkers assume that total water resistance is better than moderately high water resistance. Problems arise, however, if you ever need to disassemble any project for any reason because you cannot do so by using water as a solvent on the glue once the glue has dried. Before a full cure, it is possible to peel apart pieces glued with Titebond II with a mix of warm water and vinegar. When it has dried, a chisel is needed. Titebond II, Titebond III, the foaming polyurethane glues, epoxy, resorcinol, and plastic resin are all pretty much water-as-solvent-proof.

Figure 1.5. Aliphatic resin glues, which include your typical white and yellow wood glues, work well for most walking stick, cane, and staff projects.

POLYURETHANE GLUE

I've tried most of the polyurethane glues and find that they're excellent for many stick and cane uses. They can be especially useful when working with dense woods or with exotics such as teak. However, they're more difficult to use than yellow glues, in part because of foaming and in part because water cleanup doesn't work, and they're much more costly. There is also the possible need for misting surfaces with water when wood is extremely dry. To mist, use a cheap sprayer, such as those that cleaners come in, and spray lightly.

While less glue is needed, there is usually no need for the kind of waterproofing that polyurethane glues provide. If you decide to make projects in this book and want to make them suitable for use below the waterline, then you want to use polyurethane; otherwise, these walking sticks, canes, and staffs simply do not need that degree of waterproofing.

EPOXY

Even though cost, toxicity, and mess are limiting factors in epoxy use, epoxies are particularly handy for many stick- and cane-making projects. In those areas where the glue itself can be used as a support for a project part, like attaching metal, buttons, or other decorations to the wood, epoxy truly stands out. Epoxies are two-part adhesives: a liquid hardener that is added to a liquid resin. Cure is by chemical reaction.

Epoxies are excellent gap fillers. Only light clamping pressure is needed, and working time is adjustable to as much as 90 minutes. Epoxy's strength is incredible, and the resulting glue line is either clear or an amber color. Epoxies won't shrink, are impervious to water and most chemicals, and offer good heat resistance. If you decide to use a wood such as teak, which doesn't bond well to itself or any other wood, epoxies simplify matters. They are made to fit about any bonding need, in moderate temperature application, and most set in under five minutes.

When using epoxy, remember to mix only as much as you can use immediately. Doing so will help keep cost down and will help reduce mess. You'll also want to wear thin plastic gloves to minimize mess (see **Figure 1.6**). Go with nitrile gloves instead of latex because nitrile ones avoid the chance of latex allergies

Figure 1.6. In addition to goggles or safety glasses, thin plastic gloves, painter's tape, acetone, mixing sticks, and mixing containers are good to have on hand when working with epoxy.

showing up, are much stronger, are sometimes reuseable, are not harmed by most solvents (unlike latex), and are available in packs of 100. For general epoxy messiness, clean up quickly with acetone (nail polish remover), keeping the gloves on. Make sure all mixing containers and sticks are disposable.

Epoxies are also very toxic, which limits their use in some shops, including mine. When you use them, ensure good ventilation and avoid skin contact. Obviously, don't take it internally. If you wash up with soap and water before the epoxy sets, it usually comes off easily.

USING GLUES

Selecting the correct glue is important, but so is how you apply the glue and clamp the parts. It's also important to work with a tight-fitting joint so there are no gaps to fill, which create thick expanses of nothing but glue and weaken the project. We want our stick and cane projects to last.

First, determine the method of application—what will you use to apply the glue? The type of glue chosen determines the method, though most glues may be applied with a brush, stick, or roller.

Next, check the joint surfaces. If the joint surface is a tight fit, clean off all dust, oil, old glue, loosened and torn grain, and chips. Any cutting that has to be done is done as close as possible to the time of gluing and assembly since delays not only encourage contamination from particles in the air, but also allow oils and resins in the wood to come to the surface.

Then, before you apply the glue, test assemble to see whether the unit can be assembled within its open time (the time it takes for the glue to set). If a glue has a ten-minute open time, assembly must be completed within that time limit. Generally, the thicker you spread the glue, the longer the open assembly time. If wood is very porous or dry, open assembly time decreases. A test assembly is always a good idea—once glue is added, correcting mistakes is messy. If mistakes creep in and glue sets, mistakes must stay.

If the test assembly takes more than the allotted time, change the method of gluing or the type of adhesive so there's enough time to complete and clamp the assembly. This should not be a problem with any walking stick, cane, or staff project in this book.

Finally, mix, where required, all adhesives according to the manufacturer's directions and as accurately as possible. Spread evenly over the surfaces to be joined, getting as smooth a coat as possible.

CLAMPS

One major use of clamps in woodworking is to hold parts together while glues bond. The other major uses are to hold parts temporarily for layout and fitting, to retain jigs and stop blocks, and to hold the workpiece on the workbench while you pound away. Essentially, how you clamp the cane during the gluing process is a factor in how well your cane will stand up to use.

There are many styles of woodworking clamps available. Many have changed in recent decades, while many others have not. Clamps are something you'll collect over the years, buying and begging as they're needed for projects. If you want to buy clamps and don't need them immediately, take the time to figure out how, how often, and where they will be used. Once that's determined, the selection of clamp type just about falls in your lap, becoming nearly (but not quite) automatic. We're going to jump right on past those clamps that are not at all useful in stick and cane making, and take a look at the ones that are (see **Figure 1.7**).

CAM CLAMPS

Cam clamps are quick-action, light-duty, light-pressure bar clamps that are close to ideal for the kind of light work involved in instrument making. For sticks, canes, and staffs, use the light-duty clamps to hold multiple laminates in the shaft. Heavier clamps are needed for curved tops. The lever that activates the cam provides only light pressure, but then most of these clamps have a bar no longer than 12 inches. They are actually available in sizes up to and past 30 inches; some come with deep throats for larger work, and many have cork or other soft facing materials on the pressure faces.

Figure 1.7. Shown here are three clamps that are useful for walking stick, cane, and staff projects. The blue-headed clamp in the foreground is a small bar clamp, the yellow-handled clamp is a spring clamp, and the clamp with orange pads is a one-handed clamp.

C-CLAMPS

C-clamps are low in cost but provide a very strong pressure in a very confined area, so they are particularly useful where lots of relatively small clamps are needed. For cane making, they are used to hold stock in the arch of the top and to hold stock to other stock in vises. C-clamps need some kind of protection between the work and the clamping surface, which also helps to spread the pressure.

HAND SCREWS

Hand screws are one of the most versatile, and also one of the most underused, types of woodworking clamp. The wood jaws and steel threads allow different angles to be readily supplied, so they are wonderful for working with non-parallel surfaces and objects. For cane making, hand screws are used to clamp any surface that is not parallel to the surface being glued, as might be the case in handles.

Sizes vary: Most common today are 4 inches to 14 inches, but some up to 24 inches are available. Rotating the handles rapidly opens and closes the jaws, and using the front screw for initial sizing works quickly. The final pressure is applied with the rear screw. Jaws must be kept clean and free of glue drippings—a bit of masking tape over each jaw is a big help during glue-up. Some people prefer to tape a piece of rubber or plastic over the tips to prevent glue build-up. Such tip covers can be reusable if cared for, cleaned, and stored.

BAND CLAMPS

One of the more useful clamps for round, octagonal, or similar shapes is the band clamp (see **Figure 1.8**). You may find some cane handle designs that are most easily glued up using band clamps. These clamps range from the light- to moderate-duty 1-inch-wide bands to bands 2 inches and more in width with heavy-duty screw adjusters to draw them up very tight. The bands are heavy nylon or canvas, and heavy-duty types can apply as much as 2800 pounds of pressure per square inch. Shorter, lighter-duty bands are usually about 10 inches long, while heavier-duty types may be twice that long, or even longer.

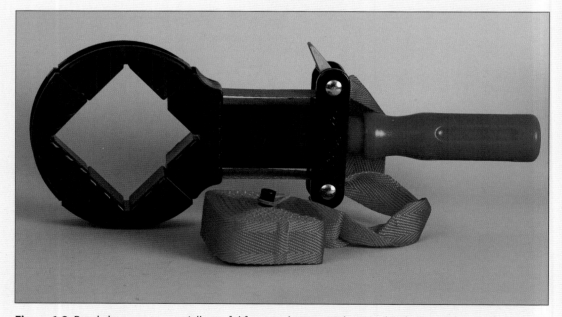

Figure 1.8. Band clamps are especially useful for round, octagonal, or similar shapes and range from light-duty to heavy-duty types. This band clamp is made for light tasks.

ONE-HANDED CLAMPS

Some years ago, quick clamps arrived on the scene and were very quickly accepted as useful in hobby shops of all kinds. The reason was, and is, simple: You can slip it closed and clamp it down with one hand, while your other hand is occupied with holding together the construct being assembled. For cane making, especially where a long shank is to be glued up, one-handed clamps provide the speed and ease needed to finish assembly before the glue sets. Pressure applied is moderate.

SPRING CLAMPS

Spring clamps are useful for many light clamping duties. For cane making, they provide speed in both clamping and unclamping, and they apply light to moderate pressure. You want either resin-bodied models or steel-bodied types.

CLAMPING AND CLAMPING PRESSURE

Clamps are used when joining wood for three reasons: Wood surfaces must be in direct and close contact with the glue; the glue must flow to a thin, continuous film; and the joint must be held steady until the glue dries. Necessary clamping pressure varies with glue type, but it usually matches glue thickness: The heavier the glue, the more clamping pressure. You need a thin, smooth glue line, not a joint squeezed dry, which may happen when too much pressure is used. It's also a good idea to set clamps within a half turn of final adjustment during a test or trial assembly. Glues have specific set times, and the closer all the assembly steps are to complete, the easier it is to finish putting it all together before the glue sets up.

Most glues used on woods fall in the intermediate pressure range, using clamp pressures of 100 to 175, even 200 pounds per square inch (psi). The pressure from a clamp is divided by the total size of the clamped area to determine the pounds per square inch being applied. Some dense hardwoods require pressures up to 300 psi. Resorcinol and urea resins require a lot of pressure; epoxy needs little or none.

To tell if you're applying the right amount of pressure, check the glue squeeze-out. Most of the time, once you get things aligned and tighten the clamps firmly so there is uniform glue squeeze-out, you'll also have applied plenty of pressure. Pay close attention to this because a clamp may apply force ranging up to a ton.

Always avoid excessive pressure in favor of uniform pressure over the entire area. Pay attention to getting uniform glue squeeze-out over the entire joint, rather than racking the project up as tight as possible. If you're turning clamp screws with pliers, you're working against yourself. Use enough clamps to get plenty of pressure without over-tightening any of them. The number of clamps needed for stick and cane joints is variable: Some people use very few clamps; others use far more. I use clamps every 8 to 10 inches with standard clamp sizes; some light clamps get spaced as close as 4 inches apart. I try never to space clamps more than 16 inches apart. If an item is only 6 to 10 inches long, I use two clamps.

Take care in cutting, assembly, and glue application, and you will get a good and long-lasting joint—provided your selection of glue follows the preceding lessons. Allow all glues and adhesives sufficient drying time—it's far better to leave clamps on too long than it is to remove them too early.

MECHANICAL FASTENERS

Mechanical fasteners range from screws to nails and back again, with variations. If the variation isn't in the screws or nails, then it is in the devices to be used with them, such as hinges, lid supports, bracing, and mending plates. Most mechanical fasteners aren't of great use in making sticks or canes, but there are some exceptionally useful types of hardware that are specially made for walking sticks, canes, and staffs.

STICK, CANE, AND STAFF TIPS

There are only a few places to get a selection of tips, and there probably aren't more than a dozen made specifically for sticks, canes, and staffs (see **Figure 1.9**). (See the Resources section on page 141.) Most important in your decision of which tip to use will be the material it's made of and its appearance.

Look for solid brass tips that offer easy installation: brass tips are often more attractive than rubber and wear longer, but they are harder to replace and more expensive at the start.

Figure 1.9. Metal can caps make great cane tips. They slip on and may be epoxied in place. A brad or small screw may also be driven into the stick's end grain to secure them.

Pick a slip-on rubber tip for security when there is some chance the cane tip might slip. Some places, such as those with soft or slick floors, do not allow metal-tipped canes.

Some tips provide a screw-on fitting for the stick bottom, and then let you choose a steel point or a rubber pad, depending on where the stick is to be used (see **Figure 1.10**). This is naturally handy for walking sticks and staffs that go indoors and outdoors often (see **Figure 1.11**). The point may be left in place if the stick is always used outdoors, and it's quick to change for indoor use.

Figure 1.10. This brass tip can be used with a spike or a rubber tip.

Tip: If you have trouble locating a tip, check any hardware store for rubber tips for chair legs. They work very well and are generally available in black, white, and brown.

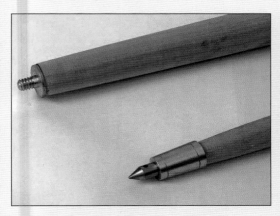

Figure 1.11. The tip on this two-part cherry walking staff is set with a spike for hiking. The spike can easily be changed to a rubber tip for indoor use.

If you decide to use a metal tip (see **Figure 1.10**), slide the tip in place and secure it with masking tape looped over its end to make sure it doesn't shift during drilling. If you decide to use a white or black rubber tip, simply remove enough wood for the tip to fit (⅞" is the inside diameter of a chair leg floor protector), and push the rubber tip on. Do not epoxy. If the tip isn't secure enough to suit you, place a dab of silicone seal on the inside of the tip and slip the stick end back in.

JOINS

Machined solid brass joins, in either ¾-inch or 1-inch diameters (see **Figure 1.12**), let you assemble two shorter lengths of a staff to make a longer one. Also look for zinc couplers, which hold the staff handle in place (see **Figure 1.13**). The coupler can be quickly removed, allowing the staff to be used as a monopod (see **Figure 1.14**) to steady a camera with longer-than-normal lenses.

Figure 1.12. Section joins are easy to use and come in two sizes, ¾" on the left and 1" on the right.

Figure 1.13. These cast zinc parts make a handle removable, leaving the slender threaded post as a camera attachment that turns the staff into a monopod.

Figure 1.14. Here is the camera attachment by itself.

Figure 1.15. Screw-on handles allow canes to be decorated very easily.

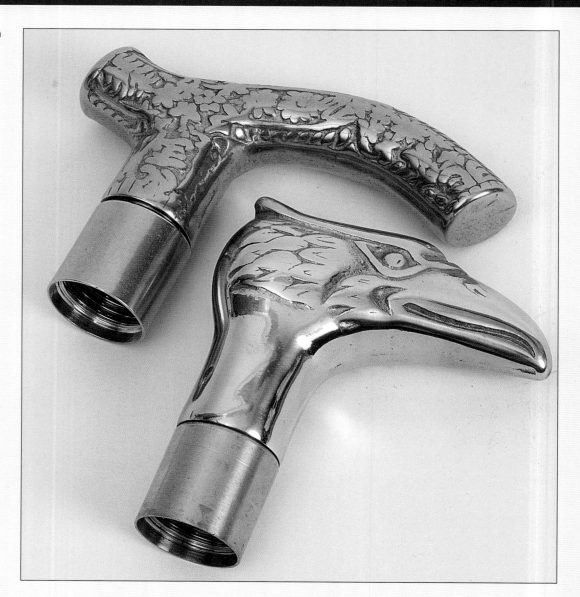

Figure 1.16. Hame knobs come in two shapes and in both brass and chrome. They make great toppers for walking sticks and staffs. The ball is held in place with a screw through a factory-drilled hole, though it may also be epoxied.

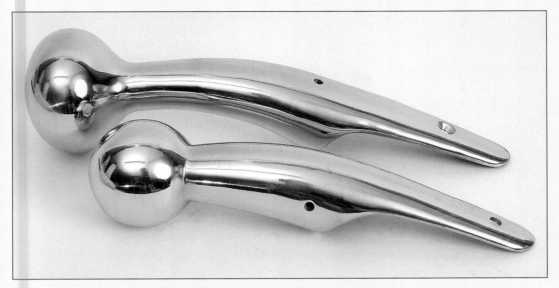

Figure 1.17. The hame ball and shaft help make it easy to create a cane. They come in different sizes and shapes.

HANDLES

Handles come in a wide variety and should be chosen to express your personality. Screw-on brass cane handles (see **Figure 1.15**) save a great deal of the time you might otherwise spend steaming and bending a crook into the wood. Steam bending works, but joined handles are easier to deal with and are much faster.

Deeper in the specialty world you'll find old-style harness trim, hame balls, and hame handles (see **Figure 1.16**). Available in different shapes and sizes, these make great knob tops for canes (see **Figure 1.17**), and they may also work nicely on walking sticks and staffs. Combine these with a short ebony shank (at ebony's price, short is desirable) and a light-colored wood for a shaft, and you can have a very effectively decorated walking staff. Make that ebony shank the basis for a camera coupler, and you've got a triple-threat walking staff.

DECORATIVE HARDWARE

Make a walking stick, cane, or staff your own by personalizing it with brass buttons, coins, and other kinds of decorative brass hardware, as shown in **Figure 1.18**. You can place these buttons and other embellishments on the tops of walking sticks, canes, or staffs. You'll most likely need to use epoxy to attach these embellishments to the wood.

Figure 1.18. Decorative items abound. Use a little imagination and you can come up with a use for old or new coins or blazer buttons like these. Upholstery tacks also work well.

SCREW TYPES

Wood screws have round, flat, and oval heads; metal screws use pan, flat, and round heads. Wood screws up to about 4 or 5 inches in length and #16 in shank size are in most hardware stores in a number of materials. Other sizes, and extremely small sizes such as ¼ inch x #0, #1, #2, #3, may have to be ordered.

Wood screws are made of mild steel, which can be coated (called zinc or galvanized) or uncoated; solid brass; or stainless steel. **Zinc-coated (galvanized) screws** and **solid brass screws** are used where corrosion is a problem. **Stainless steel screws** are best when corrosion problems are extreme, such as on or around salt water or when you need extreme strength. So, if you plan to keep any sticks and canes around salt water—on a boat, for example—use stainless steel screws.

Brass screws, the weakest of the three commonly available materials, are decorative and corrode very slowly. In probably 85 percent of projects, they're fine for stick and cane applications.

Stainless steel corrodes hardly at all but costs more. Mild steel, even zinc-plated, is the cheapest and is seldom the best solution because it will eventually rust.

Wood screws come in sizes from ¼ inch to 6 inches long. For screws to 1 inch in length, the step increase in length is ⅛ inch, while screws from 1 to 3 inches long increase in length by ¼ inch per step. Shaft sizes vary with length.

Tip: When you are countersinking, drill pilot holes at least one size smaller than the screw shank in hardwood, and two sizes in softwood. Go half to two-thirds as deep as the screw will sink.

Power drive screws, fine and coarse threaded, come in a different range of sizes than other wood screws. Power drive screws have a Phillips head, or a square drive head. With the cordless power drivers now on the market, cam-out-resisting (torque-resisting) screws, like power drive screws, are needed more than ever. Cam-out is the twisting out of the driver tip from a slot-style or other-style head (it is more likely with slotted screws) as power is applied. The new power drive screws are adapted to use with hand drivers as well as with power drivers, and the few screws in our projects are most easily driven by hand. They are exceptionally useful for light construction, including building some of the larger stick and cane projects.

Screws are not as cheap as nails, but they provide solid benefits for the extra cost. Holding strength is a lot higher. Disassembly is possible without destroying the project. Screws, however, are more work than nails to install. For many screws, only a pilot hole is needed; for flat head wood screws, countersinking is also needed. Flat head wood screws are often counterbored as well as being countersunk. The hole is filled with a flat or domed plug. Domed plugs are great for attaching wood roofing to sticks, canes, and staffs because they automatically force good water runoff at what would otherwise be a weak point.

OTHER SCREW FASTENERS

Special situations call for special fasteners, and there are a number available. Here, we'll talk about some special fasteners that are particularly useful for making sticks, canes, and staffs.

A T-nut is a threaded socket that fits into a drilled hole in wood. It is set in place and then tapped down so the teeth in the upper ring grip. The machine screw is then run into the T-nut. Ease of disassembly is built in. These are not as useful with sticks and canes as are screw inserts, but they may be useful in assembling a long walking stick or two if you wish to make your own join for the sections.

Brass screw inserts are similar to T-nuts but are screwed into a hole drilled to size. Inserts have coarse male threads on the outside and fine female threads on the inside. Brass inserts are screwed into the holes; their tops are slotted to accept a standard flat blade screwdriver tip, as shown in **Figure 1.19**. The insert is turned down until its top is flush with the surface, after which a machine screw is driven into the internal threads. Threaded inserts are also available in stainless steel.

Knurled screws may be used and are decorative. They also ease disassembly because no screwdriver is needed to install or remove them. I've used them a number of times for the simple attachment of cane shaft to cane shaft when I wanted to use short wood.

Figure 1.19. Brass screw inserts are screwed into holes, and the tops are slotted to accept a standard flat blade screwdriver tip.

TOOLS FOR WALKING STICKS, CANES, AND STAFFS

Hand tools needed for general cane and staff project construction can include anything from measuring tapes and rules to clamps and planes. A walking stick project could demand as much as a lathe or no power tools at all. We'll look at some of these tools and the general characteristics that make one more useful than another similar tool.

The tools discussed in this chapter are really all, and more than all, that is needed to make the sticks, canes, and staffs in this book. You'll also see a jig for bending cane handles, but that is described where it is used.

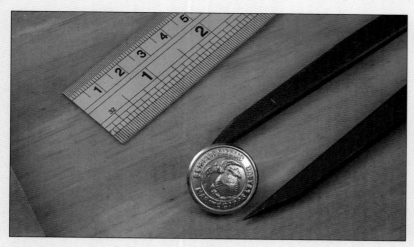

Figure 1.20. Calipers can measure round objects like this button for the top of a cane.

Figure 1.21. Measuring tapes, rules, and sliding calipers are essential and very useful.

Figure 1.22. Aluminum straightedges are accurate and easy to handle, making them a good choice for in-shop measuring. A rule may also be used to find centers.

MEASURING TOOLS

Calipers are ideal for transferring measurements from plans to wood—a basic step in any woodworking project. Good-looking, long-lasting cane and staff construction depends on accurate measurements. Calipers are ideal for measurement transfer, as shown in **Figure 1.20**. For the safety of the end user, shafts of sticks or canes need to be thick enough to be sturdy when weight is applied, so keeping measurements at specifications is essential.

> **Tip:** The basics of measuring include adding a tilt to the tape or rule when a mark is made on the workpiece. The tilt gets the blade close to the surface, instead of as much as ⅛" in the air. That air space is caused by the curl that stiffens the blade.

Measuring tapes come in many lengths and widths (see **Figure 1.21**). A 10' or 12' tape is almost always best for cane and staff makers, and usually a 6' tape is plenty—just be sure to buy the best quality. Get the best you can find with the widest tape available. The wider the tape, the stiffer it is, the longer it lasts, and the easier it is to read. Anything longer than 12 feet will be difficult to control for our stick-making purposes.

Rules and straightedges are needed in addition to a measuring tape. Folding rules tend to be unwieldy in the home shop, but some people still use them. I have a 24" aluminum straightedge, with a hardened edge, that does probably 70 percent of my in-shop measuring work, as shown in **Figure 1.22**. It is accurate, is easy to handle, and doesn't get lost as easily as all the other straightedges of lesser heft and length. A set of 12" stainless steel rules is also a help.

Figure 1.23. A sturdy straightedge is complemented by a short scribe.

Pencils, such as a standard pencil or a carpenter's pencil, make very good marks. A scribe is more precise, but the lead of a carpenter's pencil may be made to be nearly as precise and makes a mark more easily seen. Simply cut the carpenter's pencil down to a wedge, and then sand the point sharp. Keep a good sharpener around for standard pencils.

A shank awl, a scribe, or a marking knife is another option to make marks on the wood (see **Figure 1.23**) The knife actually gives the best line, which is thinner and more accurate than most other lines. Scribed lines are easier to see in dark-colored woods—just tilt the wood so the light hits the mark at an angle and you'll know where to cut.

Squares of two types are useful in making canes and staffs. The try square is a rigid frame of metal or wood and metal. A blade length of 4" to 12" is useful, with or without markings. Combination squares set depths, draw rip lines, and accomplish general tasks such as finding center on turning blanks (see **Figures 1.24** and **1.25**). Your work's quality depends on squares and how well they're used. Every shop needs a good combination square and a top-grade try square. The others are non-essentials that are sometimes nice to have.

Figure 1.24. A 6" combination square is a good size for our stick, cane, and staff projects. Combination squares set depths, draw rip lines, and do a variety of general woodworking tasks.

Figure 1.25. By connecting the corners, a combination square finds the center of a turning blank. A small square like this is a very useful measuring and layout tool.

HAND TOOLS

Canes are easily made with only the use of hand tools. Not all of the tools below are necessary, but having them on hand will make the job go quicker in most cases.

SAWS AND MITER BOXES

A ten-point panel saw and a 12" or larger hacksaw are the only two saws you'll need for our cane and staff projects. For metal or harder plastics, get a hacksaw. For rougher cuts, one of the newer hard-tooth toolbox saws, with ten points per inch, works well, cutting quickly and neatly. These two saws are the only low-cost handsaws I've seen that are worth buying. The newest versions include some finish cut saws that do a fast, clean job.

A hand miter box is a big help. For smaller-scale work, look for a miter box with an extended front that hooks onto the edge of your workbench. I've used one of these extensively in making small projects; it is a great, low-cost tool.

Figure 1.26. Bench planes, which include smooth, jack, fore, and jointer planes, are used to smooth stock.

You'll want a sharp handsaw, here being used to incise the diagonals in a turning blank so the lathe center can get a good grip.

PLANES AND BLADED HAND TOOLS

Planes command great loyalty from those who use them. But not every type of hand plane is needed for making walking sticks and canes, while several other bladed hand tools, such as spokeshaves and drawknives, are.

Bench planes (see **Figure 1.26** and **Figure 1.27**) are designed to flatten and smooth stock. The family of bench planes includes the smooth, jack, fore, and jointer types. The smallest are the smooth (also smoother, smoothing) planes, which range from 5½" to 10" long, and are used to clean up surfaces for finishing. Jack planes may be 14" or 15" long and are used to straighten and smooth large surfaces. Fore planes (18" to 20" long) are identical to, but are shorter than, jointer planes (22" to 24" long). Jointers are used for truing long edges and flattening long surfaces. All of these planes work well for the basic shaping of the wood you will use for your sticks, canes, or staffs.

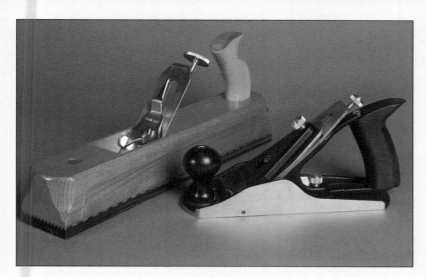

Figure 1.27. Smooth planes, like the two shown here, are the smallest of the bench planes and are used for smoothing stock before finishing.

CHECKING PLANE QUALITY

In hand planes, most of the features that illustrate good quality (or better) are obvious: good fit, good finish, sturdy design, top materials. But if you don't know planes, you might miss some necessary features.

Look for a small mouth. The smaller the plane's mouth, the lower the possibility of wood tear-out. Look for an adjustable toe, the edge just in front of the front of the blade, so that you can adjust the mouth to cut the shaving thickness you wish.

Look for a flat sole. The sole should be highly finished, whether iron or wood, and as flat as possible. On wooden planes, flattening the sole may be a recurring job, depending on the type of wood used.

Let use determine sole length. If you're jointing or smoothing long boards, you want a long plane so it stays up out of the dips and gives you a truly flat, smooth surface.

Make sure the shape of the sole matches the iron. If you have a straight iron, the sole must also be straight. If the iron is convex, then the sole must be convex, concave if concave, and so on. Scrub planes are an exception; they usually have a curved iron with a flat sole, for removing a lot of wood in a hurry.

Check the fit of the tote, or rear handle. It should fit the hand well. A poor fit on any handle must be corrected because the bad fit will raise blisters on your hands.

Check the knob. The knob, or front handle, probably will be either a horn type (European pattern wood planes, among others) or a ball type (American metal planes). On newer planes, the ball is made of molded plastic, and the mold seam will not have been removed. You can remove the seam, buy a new handle set, or turn yourself a new handle out of whatever wood you prefer.

Check the cutter. A single iron is often a sign of a cheap plane, but it just as often indicates a design where a back iron isn't workable. In a double iron, the top curling iron serves as a chip breaker so that shavings break and curl upward, reducing or eliminating splintering and tear-out. A double iron also helps cut down on blade chatter.

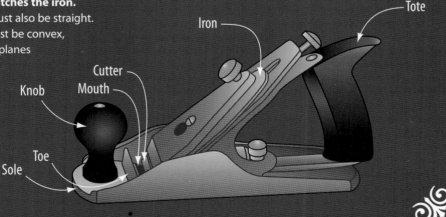

Block planes are short planes with low-angle irons (see **Figure 1.28** and **Figure 1.29**)—most of the time. Usually, block plane irons are set at 20 or 21 degrees with the bevel up so their cutting angle remains around 45 degrees. Some special block planes have irons bedded at an angle of 12 degrees, though, with the bevel up, their cutting angle is still around 35 degrees. The regular block plane works fine on the end grain of softer woods, while the low-angle plane is needed for harder woods.

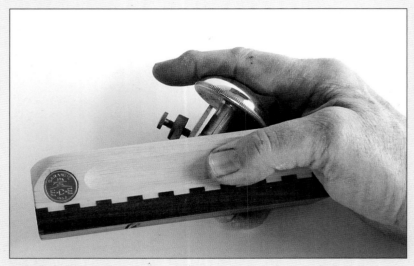

Figure 1.28. Typically, a block plane is a short plane with a low-angle iron and is used for general smoothing, even on end grain. This particular one has a wooden body.

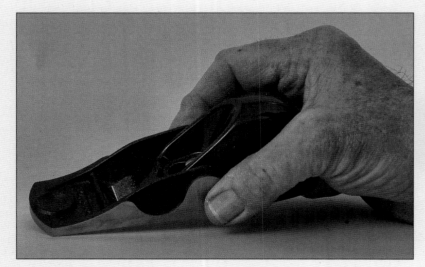

Figure 1.29. This plane is another example of a block plane, only it has a metal body.

Scrub planes may be classed as bench planes. Bodies are 9½" to 10½" long, and the irons will be either 1¼" or 1½" wide with a pronounced curve. Besides the curved, thick, single iron, the main difference between the scrub plane and the wider bench plane is in the size of the mouth: Scrub planes have large mouth openings to allow loads of waste to get through easily. Use the scrub plane to remove a lot of wood, usually by planing at an angle in between going with the grain and going across it.

Router planes flatten the bottom of recessed areas, which today is often done with a flat-bottom router bit. They are very handy for cleanups and touch-ups on machine-routed areas, as well as for cutting their own patterns (see **Figure 1.30**).

Spokeshaves trim or form square wood into other shapes, so they're very useful in making sticks and canes. The spokeshave is available with a flat knife, with a hollow shave (curving outward and down from the handle), and with a round shave (see **Figure 1.31**), used for forming rounds or dowels. The flat sole works to round stock and can bevel edges quite easily. The name indicates the tool's use: It was once, and occasionally still is, used for shaping the spokes of wagon wheels. Spokeshaves are used with either a push or a pull stroke, depending on which seems to give the most control.

Tip: To get a clean shear when working corners with a spokeshave, try pulling the shave at an angle.

Figure 1.30. Router planes flatten the bottom of recessed areas or can clean up machine-routed areas. This particular plane has a nice wooden body.

Rasps are available in flat, half-round, and round styles. A rasp is similar to a file, but it is meant for cutting materials softer than steel, such as wood and hoof, and provides a fast and easy method to size and shape project parts. For cane, stick, and staff shaft work, the flat and half-round rasps are useful.

A **drawknife** is a shaving or chamfering knife (see **Figure 1.32**). It can cut wood to a finished shape very nicely, but it may also be used to remove bark without cutting far, if at all, into the wood itself. For greatest control and most precise results, keeping the bevel down works best, but if you really want to hog out some wood, put the bevel up. When you get close to your mark, turn the bevel down and get precise.

Figure 1.31. This is a convex surface spokeshave, used to form round surfaces.

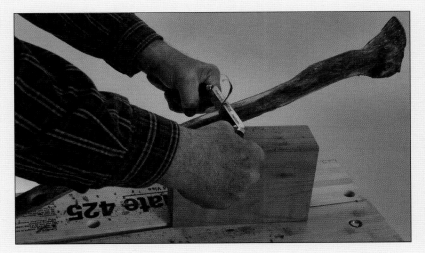

Figure 1.32. For walking sticks, canes, and staffs, the drawknife is particularly useful for removing bark without taking away much of the wood itself.

ADDITIONAL HAND TOOLS

A 10 or 13 ounce hammer will serve our purposes. Hammers are available in many styles and sizes, but, for our cane and staff projects, this is the only hammer you'll need. Handle materials include hickory or fiberglass, as well as solid and tubular steel. There are advantages to each: Wood costs less and absorbs shock beautifully; fiberglass is easiest on the hand and forearm; steel is strongest. Make sure the hammer handle is securely attached to its head.

A screwdriver should be selected for head style and for quality. They come in all the obvious head styles to fit old and new head patterns. A good screwdriver handle fits your hand well, and good blades are of alloys that last. Look for tip machining that is clean and neat. For me, the best-handling screwdrivers are those with more or less cone-shaped handles that fit the hand. Newer models may also have a soft plastic grip for the handle so your hand slips less. For most uses, a square drive works best, reduces torquing out to almost nothing, and is becoming ever more popular. A power driver, even a low-powered one, is overkill when running a 1½"-long #6 screw into end grain.

> **Tip:** Make your tools last longer: use them for their intended purpose. Screwdrivers are frequently abused tools. Don't use yours as levers or awls unless you enjoy replacing them more often than need be.

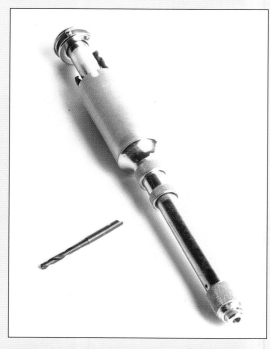

Figure 1.33. A push drill is simple and quick to use.

Figure 1.34. A brad point drill bit will start without an initial center punch and makes a clean hole.

A **push drill or hand drill** is a tool you may or may not be interested in. With today's array of cordless drills, almost no one bothers with hand drills. At the same time, push drills (see **Figure 1.33**) and hand drills are excellent ways to get a few pilot holes drilled quickly without any worry about batteries or extension cords and with hardly any risk of a damaging slip.

DRILL BITS

A good-quality brad point drill bit set is necessary. Brad point bits (see **Figure 1.34**) come in sizes from ³⁄₁₆" to 1" in most sets. Brad points allow easy starting without center punching, and the bits cut a nice, clean hole that is ideal for doweling.

Forstner bits (see **Figure 1.35**) are also a consideration for stick and cane makers. These bits cut an exceptionally clean hole with a flat bottom. Top-quality Forstner bits are expensive, but, for clean work, they're worth it. Sizes over 1" aren't needed for canes and staffs. Don't bother looking for sizes smaller than ¼"; due to the Forstner bit configuration, ¼" is the smallest size made. If you are using a handheld drill, be sure that you use a Forstner bit with a center spur. If you have Forstner bits without a center spur, they must be used in a drill press.

Twist bits are good for drilling pilot holes for screws (see **Figure 1.36**).

Tip: To get the best use from any drill bit when drilling through holes, clamp or otherwise affix a backing board where the drill bit will exit the wood. This reduces splintering, resulting in a clean hole. This technique works with any drill bit.

Tip: Forstner bits hold heat because of their heavy heads, so they must be run at slow speeds. They work best if backed off and cooled down on deep holes.

Tip: Most versions of the Forstner bit don't have much of a starting spur; cutting starts on the rim. This makes the centering of holes fairly difficult, unless you use them in a drill press.

Figure 1.35. Forstner bits make clean, flat-bottomed holes.

Figure 1.36. Twist bit sets will cover the whole range of pilot holes.

Power tools

For the most part, power tools are optional for our cane and staff projects. A lathe, of course, is our one essential power tool because we will be turning some of our sticks round on it. The other tools mentioned here can make some tasks easier or faster, but they are certainly not necessary to complete the projects in this book.

LATHE

The lathe is an essential tool for some of our cane and stick projects because it allows you to turn and finish a beautiful tapered shaft, as you can see in **Figures 1.37** and **Figure 1.38**.

Figure 1.37. The lathe allows you to remove wood quickly and accurately to form round stock for your stick, cane, and staff projects.

Figure 1.38. The lathe also makes it easier to smooth out the shafts of sticks, canes, and staffs. Here, the skew chisel makes a planing cut and leaves a very smooth surface.

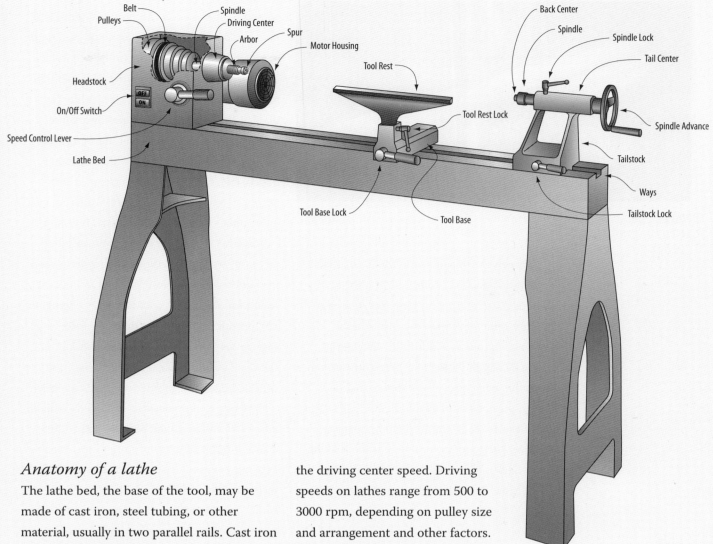

Belt
Spindle
Pulleys
Driving Center
Arbor
Spur
Motor Housing
Headstock
On/Off Switch
Speed Control Lever
Lathe Bed
Tool Rest
Back Center
Spindle
Spindle Lock
Tail Center
Spindle Advance
Tool Rest Lock
Tailstock
Ways
Tool Base Lock
Tool Base
Tailstock Lock

Figure 1.39. A lathe is essential for some of the projects in this book. Shown here are parts that are common to many lathes.

Anatomy of a lathe

The lathe bed, the base of the tool, may be made of cast iron, steel tubing, or other material, usually in two parallel rails. Cast iron is considered better than tubing because it is heavier. The more solid the bed, the more accurate the lathe. Other things being equal, the heavier a lathe is, the more precisely you can turn with it. Weight dampens vibration, and vibration is the enemy of smooth turning.

The machined parts of the bed, on which the tool rest and the tailstock move, are the ways (see **Figure 1.39**). Whether the bed is tubing, cast iron, or other material, accurate machining and great strength are necessary.

At the left end of the bed is the headstock, which may also contain the motor housing. The driving center, with spur, attaches to an arbor that holds a pulley that leads through a series of belts to the motor. Swap the belts from pulley to pulley and you raise and lower the driving center speed. Driving speeds on lathes range from 500 to 3000 rpm, depending on pulley size and arrangement and other factors. Slow speeds are for large work, high speeds for small work. Some newer lathes do not use belts, but provide an electronic speed control that is both fast and safe to use (some turners tend to not always wait for the pulleys to stop moving before starting to shift belts, which may be rough on the fingers).

At the far end of the lathe is the tailstock. This part moves along the base rails to vary the distance between the back center and the driving center so different-length workpieces may be turned. The tailstock has a spindle lock that holds the tail center and a spindle advance to help lock pieces in place for turning, and there is a tailstock lock, usually located under the tailstock, between the rails.

Figure 1.40. Spindle turning on the lathe is aided by a steady rest. There are several on the market. This one is homemade.

Between the tailstock and the headstock is the tool rest. This adjustable platform, in various shapes (straight, long, short, S, and V are just some), is where the turner rests the turning tool as it shaves away material. The tool rest has a lock for height and distance from the work, plus a lock that holds the rest in position on the lathe bed. Some lathes also have a steady rest for helping manage slender workpieces, a real help when making canes, though you can make one for yourself (see **Figure 1.40**) and you can also learn how to do without one.

Turning tools

Turning tools look a lot like chisels, but they have longer handles and shanks plus blunter tips. Primary shapes for spindle-turning tools are the skew, the gouge, the parting tool, and the scraper. Beading tools may also be handy in decorating shafts.

OTHER POWER TOOLS

As I mentioned earlier, power tools are not really necessary to make walking sticks, canes, or staffs. However, the list below notes some power tools that are helpful to have on hand.

A table saw provides great versatility and accuracy in cutting. Table saws come in a wide range of types, sizes, and styles. As with so many other woodworking tools, there is a plethora of options, and you should be able to suit your needs and budget pretty accurately. There's not much sense buying a big cabinet saw if all you'll ever do are projects like the ones in this book. At the same time, some of the super-cheap table saws are inaccurate enough to make good results darned near impossible. Choose first for size, next for accuracy, and last for weight, considering cost as it applies to your cane and staff building.

A router is used for rounding over billets of wood (wood that is square or nearly square in cross section and long enough to make at least part of a shaft), creating fancy edging, and producing joints like dovetails (see **Figure 1.41**). For cane and staff making, they're handiest for making sure edges are rounded over and splinter free. Pick a model with about 1½ horsepower, preferably with an adaptable collet to take both ½" and ¼" bits. There is quite an array of router bits available. I strongly suggest that you buy bits as needed instead of buying large sets. Sets of mixed router bits tend to waste money because as many as half may never be used. A plunge router is handy, though far from essential for most work.

For cane and stick making, a **router table** makes it easy to create complex edging and molding parts for projects because cut depths are more easily maintained. Router tables are essential for the widest router use and greatly extend precision and possibilities. A good router table turns a router into a small shaper and keeps you from needing special jigs for each action.

A compound miter saw can speed work and remove complexity from angle cuts and straight end cuts (see **Figure 1.42**). A laser-equipped model helps with marking the exact point of cut.

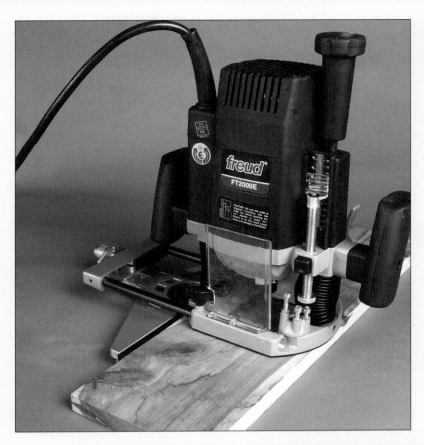

Figure 1.41. A plunge router with an edge guide can do a lot of the work on canes and staffs.

Figure 1.42. Here, a 10" slide compound miter saw is squaring a board end.

Figure 1.43. The band saw's tilting table can be handy for preshaping handles for staffs.

Figure 1.44. A thickness planer smoothes rough wood and makes it uniform in thickness. You can save money by surfacing your own wood.

Band saws are great for cutting curves in thick material (see **Figure 1.43**), for pattern cutting or sanding, and for resawing to reduce the thickness of boards without using a planer. They're also handy for stack cutting, a method in which you tape pieces of wood together and cut them all at the same time. This saves time for anyone making more than one of a single pattern. Most 14" and larger band saws can cut several pieces at one time (depending on thickness), in almost any kind of wood.

The planer and jointer are used to put square and flat faces and edges on boards. Generally, 6" and 8" jointers are considered suitable in size, cost, and utility for home workshops. The portable planer has helped make planing more affordable for the home hobby shop, but you'll have to sit down and figure out if the ability to thickness woods quickly and accurately is of great importance in your work. You'll find planers especially useful if you choose to buy unsurfaced wood (see **Figure 1.44**), which is a great way to save money (see the Planing for Cheaper Wood sidebar on page 14).

EYE, HEARING, AND LUNG SAFETY

Whether you use hand or power tools, protect your eyes, hearing, and lungs while woodworking. Use standard and common sense safety rules as well.

Eye protection must always be worn while working with most woodworking tools, whether it's safety glasses (see **Figure 1.45**), safety goggles, or a face shield. Safety glasses, goggles, and face shields must meet ANSI (American National Standards Institute) standards.

Hearing protectors keep high-volume, high-frequency sounds away from the eardrums. Among the worst sound emitters are small planers, routers, and some vacuum cleaners. Loud jobs require hearing protectors,

and most power woodworking jobs come under that heading. The longer you are exposed, the more harmful those sounds are. Both insert- and muff-type protectors are available. Look for an EPA (Environmental Protection Agency) noise-reduction rating (NRR) of at least 25 decibels (db).

For dust-producing projects, use a dust mask. Disposable dust masks are good for keeping dust and fine solid particles from being inhaled. Some masks have a filter pad and holder with a strap to hold the mask over the nose and mouth. Others are formed shapes of filter material.

Remember to keep yourself out of harm's way and use common sense. For example, make sure the router remains in or on the work until the bit stops turning after the switch is turned off. If that uncovered bit is not moving when it touches you, it only makes small cuts.

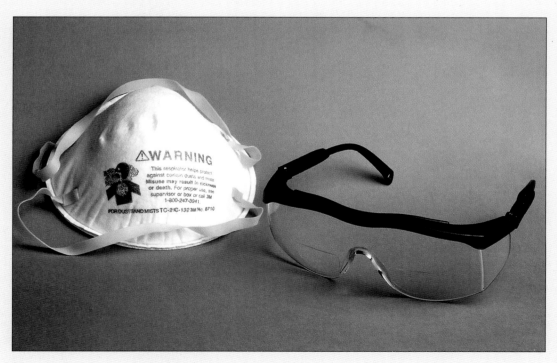

Figure 1.45. A dust mask and safety glasses are two of the most essential safety devices for any kind of woodworking; remember to protect your ears with hearing protectors and your limbs with common sense.

FINISHES FOR WALKING STICKS, CANES, AND STAFFS

The high sheen of a super-gloss clear finish is as wonderful on walking sticks, canes, and staffs as it is on pianos. On our projects, it is easy to apply, it gives as much protection as we need, and it can be an interior or exterior variety, since either works. If you'd rather have a low-luster sheen, check out satin exterior finishes.

Canes can also be painted or stained. Paint or stain can be decorative, but it can also be practical. If you don't wish to buy expensive and fancy woods and don't have them on hand, you can use woods with a plain grain, such as soft maple or tulip poplar, and cover the plain grain with an appropriate color of paint or enamel.

Choosing the right finish is probably the hardest part of finishing walking sticks, canes, and staffs. There are some basic similarities among different types of finish, but also some major differences, most depending on what you decide is the best combination of durability, ease of application, and appearance. Generally, ease of application is more important than durability for outdoor clear finishes since you probably are not going to store your canes and walking sticks outdoors. Appearance is always subjective, so you've got to judge for yourself what you like the most after trying a few types and brands. Let's take a look at what's involved in finishing a cane in a step-by-step order.

Figure 1.46. ZAR produces both brush-on and spray finishes. These are polyurethanes that withstand a great deal of wear and weather.

Figure 1.47. Danish and teak oils, like these from Woodworker's Supply, are easy finishes to apply. They're not as durable as polyurethane varnish, but another coat is easy to add at almost any time.

THE FINISHING PROCESS

Finishes for walking sticks, canes, and staffs do not have to be complex. If you wish, you can use the latest HVLP (High Volume Low Pressure) gear and do a fancy job, spending hours rubbing out each finish, but, unless you're preparing sticks for a show, that's likely to be time and money wasted. The following steps will give you an idea of the different finishing techniques you can employ, and you may elect to skip steps that don't apply to your particular finish. You can find specific instructions for the finishes used on the projects included with each project.

STEP ONE: SELECTING A CLEAR FINISH

It is the wide selection of clear finishes that complicates the finishing procedure. You'll want to select the clear finish as your first step to be sure that it won't interact with any of the other products you plan to use. Generally, remember that most oil finishes, such as teak oil and Danish oil, can be coated with almost any final finish—from shellac to polyurethane. Polyurethanes can be very difficult to recoat over themselves without a lot of sanding, and they do not accept other finishes as covers very well.

Here's a quick review of some of the different products. Under normal circumstances, any good semi-gloss or high-gloss exterior finish does very well.

- Polyurethane gives a super-sturdy finish, but be sure its formula is UV-resistant for exterior durability. This is true of any clear exterior finish; otherwise, the film can break down in less than a single season.
- UGL's ZAR water-based polyurethane finish (see **Figure 1.46**) gives excellent

protection. Among its good points are the water cleanup and quick drying time—recommended time to recoating is two hours, which means you can lay three coats a day on a walking stick and have it ready to go before you fold up and head out for the Saturday night movie. And it comes in satin, so you don't have to break a gloss finish with #0000 steel wool to get rid of glare.

- Minwax makes several satin luster products that are really excellent.
- Oils such as Danish, tung, and teak are also worth trying on your canes (see **Figures 1.47** and **1.48**). They do not make thick films; rather, they penetrate the wood and bring out the figure.
- Wax also makes an interesting finish that is very easy to renew (see **Figure 1.49**).

WEATHER AND HUMIDITY

Extreme warmth, as in summer, presents less of a problem for applying finishes than does extreme winter cold. Most finishes flow on decently in temperatures above 90ºF and cure properly, but they don't cure well below 60ºF even if they don't clump on the brush or rag or in the spray gun.

Humidity is a controllable factor in shops and homes, but it is not always one that is controlled. The more coats of finish, the better the reduction of moisture movement and the less effect moisture has on the wood parts of any project. Keeping humidity to rational levels within the shop—upwards of 35 percent and under 55 percent, for example—is fairly easy to do, but you retain no control of humidity once a project leaves your hands, so it makes sense to make it as resistant to airborne moisture as possible.

Figure 1.48. Tung oil goes on very easily with a lint-free rag.

Figure 1.49. Waxes make an interesting finish for canes and walking staffs. Simply apply and buff until you have the sheen you wish. If it dims later on, add another application and buff again.

Figure 1.50. This is a classic quarter sheet finish sander from Porter-Cable and does most finishing quite well.

STEP TWO: PREPARING THE SURFACES

Before you apply a finish, make sure the surfaces are clean, dry, and sanded to the smoothness available with 150-grit sandpaper. The wide array of random orbit sanders and finishing sanders available today take most of the grief out of finish sanding: They sand to a fine finish without leaving swirl marks, and they quickly reduce badly marred material to near perfection (see **Figure 1.50**). For turned canes or sticks, you can do the sanding while the stick is still on the lathe (see **Figure 1.51**), though not when steam bending is needed as well.

Complete your cane or stick right through hardware installation. Then remove the hardware. Use a two- or three-step sanding process. If the wood is smooth to start, two steps may work well. If the wood is rough, use three, or even four, steps. Start with 100-grit sandpaper, depending on surface quality, as

Figure 1.51. Sanding is an essential preparation for every type of finish on wood. On-lathe sanding saves a great deal of time and works better than trying to hand sand or power sand with the shaft off the lathe.

mentioned earlier; use 150-grit sandpaper for a medium finish, which is all that's suitable for some sticks (twisted natural willow, sumac, and similar woods). Vacuum the surface. Wipe it down very carefully with a tack cloth.

STEP THREE: USING FILLERS

Prepping a piece of wood to get a smooth coat of paint, and sometimes stain, is essential, especially with enamels that are fairly thin and don't fill in all that well. There are several choices of sanding sealer or filler available if sandpaper doesn't create a smooth surface (see **Figure 1.52**), as it will not on open-pored woods like red oak or walnut. I usually use a sanding sealer to fill the worst surface whorls in the wood and then come back over it with a 180- or 220-grit sandpaper. Two or three coats of sealer may be needed on some hardwoods. Some woods, usually open-grain hardwoods like ash and oak, may require more work: You may choose to use an auto body filler on these. Bondo or its counterparts need one coat—wipe on, wipe off, and sand to 180 or 220 grit.

Figure 1.52. Grain fillers help smooth wood, especially when paints or stain don't fill well.

Figure 1.53. These ZAR stains are heavily pigmented, wipe on and off easily, and do a fine job of adding color to lighter woods.

STEP FOUR: APPLYING COLOR

If you don't want to add color, simply skip ahead to applying the clear finish.

If you want to apply stain, use a clean brush or a clean lint-free cloth. Use a penetrating stain for best appearance (see **Figure 1.53**). I prefer semi-transparent to opaque for the same reason I prefer penetrating over non-penetrating: The opaque and non-penetrating stains block the character of the wood. Stains are best used to enhance the color and figure of wood. Give stain about 15 to 20 minutes to penetrate, and wipe off any excess. For many projects, you'll reach one end of the coating job just as you need to go back and wipe off the excess from the earlier parts of the work. Let any stain dry no less than six hours, preferably overnight. If you want a darker color, lightly go over the surfaces with

#0000 steel wool or 220-grit sandpaper and repeat the staining process. After twelve hours, you can safely figure on applying your first clear finish coating.

If you want to finish with paint, start by applying the first coat of enamel and letting it dry. This coat will give you an idea of how much more sanding is needed and how many more coats are needed. Proceed with more coats, sanding lightly between coats with 320-grit sandpaper for finest results. Make sure you don't sand through the finish.

For general stick use, you'll probably go no further than three coats with very light sanding between coats, especially with spray enamels, such as Krylon, which dry so rapidly you can lay on successive coats at five- or ten-minute intervals. Brush-on enamels are thicker, though still thin compared to some latex paints, and require fewer coats. I don't feel that a heavy brush enamel gives a decent-looking painted finish on sticks and canes, but these enamels may be thinned and sprayed, though they may take more pressure than a small sprayer can produce.

Be sure any paint or stain dries completely before you add your clear finish.

Tip: If you're going to apply a second or third coat of stain on a piece the next day and want to keep using the same cloth wipe, get a clean glass jar, place the cloth inside, and store it in the refrigerator overnight. This keeps the cloth from drying out and allows you to continue using the same prepared applicator.

STEP FIVE: APPLYING THE CLEAR FINISH

Clear finish application is simple, but it's easy to mess it up. Clean up your stick carefully, and use a tack cloth so there are no bits of steel wool left behind to rust and create bumps in the finish. Modern safety directions say you shouldn't use a blast of air to clean out nooks and crannies in a project. Presumably, this adds sanding dust and steel wool particles to the air, creating eventual lung problems. Use a good shop vacuum instead and follow with the tack cloth.

Apply the first coat of finish with a clean cloth made from an old T-shirt or diaper, a top-quality brush, or a spray system. Cover all sides and edges of the project with an equal number of coats. Lay on any successive coats the same way, allowing plenty of drying time between coats (check the finish manufacturer's instructions). You can check finish application for adequate coverage and see how much of the surface has dried by using a portable light placed at a low angle to the work surface.

Continue to apply coats of clear finish until you're satisfied with the finish, which could be three coats or ten. Once the final coat is fully dry, replace the hardware.

WALKING STICK, CANE, AND STAFF PROJECTS

PART · 2

You can craft your walking stick, cane, or staff in a variety of styles. This section includes directions for 15 projects, arranged from easiest to hardest. The easiest style is the flat walking stick: These projects require only basic shop tools to create. Bark-on sticks show the natural beauty of found wood. The willow stick projects demonstrate how to remove bark from natural sticks and showcase some of the wood's unique characteristics. A section of carving patterns is included to help you take some of the projects to the next level. Turned sticks are a step up in difficulty, as they require a lathe. Lamination can create bends and can create canes from multiple species of wood. Once you have tried all of the different types or just your favorites, you'll have the tools you need to create your own custom projects.

FLAT WALKING STICKS

Flat walking sticks—made from regular lumber—are the easiest projects by far in the book, with need for the fewest tools.

One white oak project, one of mesquite, and two of sycamore are demonstrated here. The woods are interchangeable and many other species are suitable, including some softwoods. These are the walking sticks you'll find at craft fairs selling for upwards of ten dollars.

The following projects are all created from the same pattern. The variety of woods and finishing techniques used in the projects reveals the versatility of even the simplest walking stick design. Working through the projects in this section will also give you practice making modifications to a design to suit your preferences and available materials.

FLAT WALKING STICK IN WHITE OAK

This first project is the basis for the other walking sticks shown in this section, and the process for creating it is simple—we'll be cutting the stick to shape and then sanding and finishing it. A great beginning project, this stick requires very few tools to make and is a great way to build confidence because its easy-to-make process produces a nice end result.

I've used white oak because it is a durable wood, so this stick may be propped outside the back door and left in the weather without coming to any harm for quite a long time.

I've provided a pattern for cutting out the white oak handle on a band saw or a scroll saw. With the rounded top and the slant for the tip, there is probably 15 minutes of labor in this project, not counting finishing time. Of course, the project could be left unfinished.

Purchase a 1" x 6" white oak board at your local lumber mill. Begin by making sure the board is planed to ¾" thick (for nominal 1" sizes, ¾" is the standard finished size). Next, rip to 2½" wide on a table saw. If you don't have a table saw, most lumberyards will rip to width at your request for a small charge. Select a length you feel will be comfortable, from about 42" to 54", and cut to length (see Sizing Walking Sticks and Canes on page 25).

The Flat Walking Stick in White Oak is made from flat lumber. It takes just a few minutes to saw and shape.

MATERIALS

- ○ White oak, ¾" thick and 2½" wide, length to fit
- ○ Copy of pattern on page 69
- ○ 10', 12', or 16' measuring tape
- ○ Band saw, scroll saw, or coping saw
- ○ Wood rasp
- ○ Patternmaker's rasp
- ○ Power sander (optional)
- ○ Sandpaper in 80, 100, and 120 grits
- ○ Finish of your choice (I used wax.)

Saw the handle—Copy the pattern on any copying machine. It is full-size. Place the pattern on the handle area, tape lightly, and saw with a band saw, scroll saw, or coping saw. Remove the pattern.

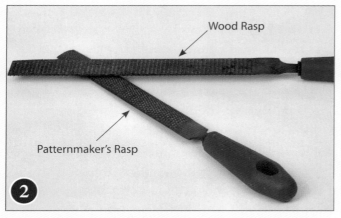

Wood Rasp

Patternmaker's Rasp

Taper the tip—Saw the tapers on the tip starting at 3½" up from the bottom and 1" in from each side using a band saw, scroll saw, or coping saw. Clean them up using a wood rasp to rough in and a patternmaker's rasp to finish size. To get a sharper tip, you can use any power sander to quickly remove the excess material.

Sand and finish—Sand the entire stick lightly, starting at the coarsest grit and moving to the finest. You may hand or power sand, so choose whichever method is most comfortable. Then, wax, or apply the stain and finish of your choice.

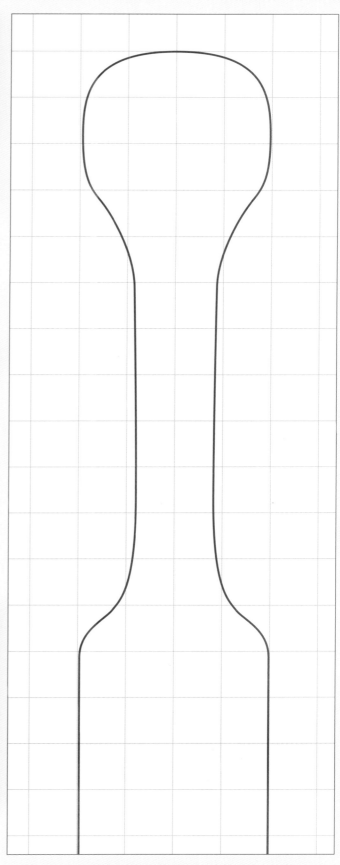

Use this full-size pattern for the flat walking stick handle. Each square equals ½".

The wood in the flat sycamore stick has a bright glow.
When quarter sawn, it has a nice lacy figure.

FLAT WALKING STICK IN SYCAMORE

This second project is very similar to the Flat Walking Stick in White Oak on page 68, only here we're using sycamore instead of white oak. In this demonstration, we'll be learning how to make some slight modifications to allow for the hardness of the wood.

Sycamore is an underrated and underused wood, in my eyes anyway. It has a great-looking, lacy figure in quarter-sawn billets and is quite stable when quarter sawn. Don't purchase flat-sawn pieces because sycamore shifts shape like crazy when flat sawn.

Purchase a 1" x 6" sycamore board from your local lumberyard. Use your table saw to rip ¾" stock to about 2½" in width. Mark for the desired length, from as little as 42" on up past 54", if desired (see Sizing Walking Sticks and Canes on page 25). After rasping the handle smooth and giving it an overall sanding, this walking stick got three coats of teak oil as a finish. A variation, as seen in the next project, is to use a hame ball as a top knob.

MATERIALS

- ○ Quarter-sawn sycamore, ¾" thick and 2½" wide, length to fit
- ○ Copy of pattern on page 69
- ○ 10', 12', or 16' measuring tape
- ○ Band saw, scroll saw, or coping saw
- ○ Wood rasp
- ○ Patternmaker's rasp
- ○ Power sander (optional)
- ○ Sandpaper, 80, 100, and 120 grit
- ○ Finish of your choice (I used teak oil.)

Saw the handle—Use the same pattern for the handle as for the previous project, the Flat Walking Stick in White Oak. You can modify the top dome into a flat shape or a different curve, but the overall size and handgrip thickness should be the same.

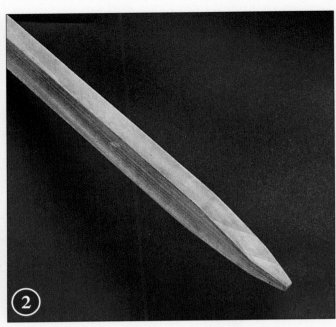

Cut the tip—Cut the tip slightly blunt because sycamore is a softer hardwood than white oak. Cut your angle from 3½" up the shaft to about ⅜" out on each side, and, if desired, sand for a slightly more pointed tip.

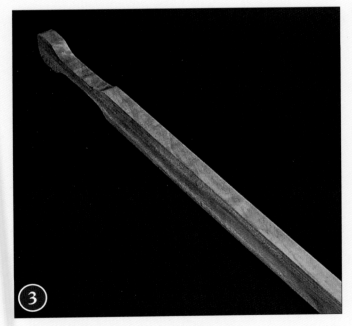

Finish—Apply teak oil or use the finish of your choice.

FLAT WALKING STICK IN SYCAMORE WITH HAME BALL

This second sycamore walking stick shares a lot of features with the first because it was cut from the same board at around the same time. In this project, we'll be using stain for a finish and learning how to add hardware for our top. To make this stick, leave off the top and replace the handle with a hame ball for a completely different look.

MATERIALS

- ○ Quarter-sawn sycamore, ¾" thick and 2½" wide, length to fit
- ○ Band saw, scroll saw, or coping saw
- ○ Wood rasp
- ○ Patternmaker's rasp
- ○ Power sander (optional)
- ○ Sandpaper, 80, 100, and 120 grits
- ○ Finish of your choice (I used ZAR charcoal stain and Minwax Wipe-On Poly.)
- ○ Hame ball
- ○ Screwdriver to fit #4 x ¾" solid brass screw
- ○ Screw, #4 x ¾" solid brass
- ○ Epoxy

Staining the sycamore in this flat walking stick gives the wood a rich color that really brings out the ray flecks in the quarter-sawn surface.

Make the stick—Make this walking stick by following the same basic steps for the Flat Walking Stick in White Oak on page 69. Instead of cutting out the handle pattern, cut a shaft to mount the hame ball on. You can rasp the edges off to create a rounded shaft or leave it as is, but be sure to match the final size of the shaft end to the diameter of the opening in your hame ball. Then, taper the tip using the wood rasp and the patternmaker's rasp. Sand the stick before moving on to finishing.

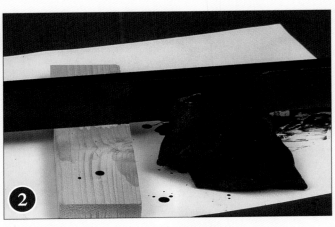

Stain the stick—I wanted to stain the sycamore to bring out the ray flecks, so I used ZAR charcoal stain. The photos show the beginning of applying the stain and following wiping off the stain after about 15 minutes.

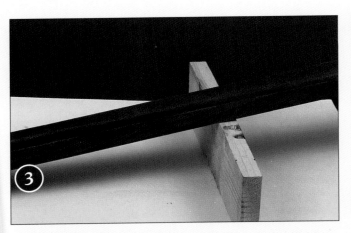

Protect the stick—The stained wood was coated with a polyurethane reinforced oil, in this case Minwax Wipe-On Poly. Three coats of that protect against anything the stick is likely to encounter.

Glue the ball—The tip of the handle end was left clean, or without finish, so that the epoxy used to secure the hame ball could get a good grip on the wood. Use the appropriate screwdriver to drive a small screw through the hole in the ball collar into the shaft, further securing it.

Mesquite is a very hard and durable wood with beautiful luster. It also can be badly checked and prone to cracking.

FLAT WALKING STICK IN MESQUITE

For this last flat walking stick project, we'll be using yet a different wood—mesquite—to get some experience with a wood that is more difficult to work. Mesquite is the most durable wood found in the United States. It is expensive, but it finishes beautifully and easily, sands like a dream, and generally provides a lot of pleasure with the finished results. It can, however, be a tricky wood to work with. Highly figured pieces tend to break. Be sure to make your stick a bit wider than the pattern calls for to avoid this problem.

In the photo in Step 4, you see the teak-oil finished mesquite walking stick leaning on a mesquite turning block, which shows the contrast between the finished and unfinished wood. Both started with pretty much the same color and figure.

MATERIALS

- ○ Mesquite, ¾" thick and 2½" wide, length to fit
- ○ Copy of pattern on page 69
- ○ 10', 12', or 16' measuring tape
- ○ Band saw, scroll saw, or coping saw
- ○ Wood rasp
- ○ Patternmaker's rasp
- ○ Power sander (optional)
- ○ Sandpaper, 100 and 120 grit
- ○ Finish of your choice (I used teak oil.)

Cut the mesquite—Using a pattern much like the one on page 69, cut the mesquite to about 2½" width, cut the handle shape, and cut the tip at an angle like that on the Flat Walking Stick in Sycamore.

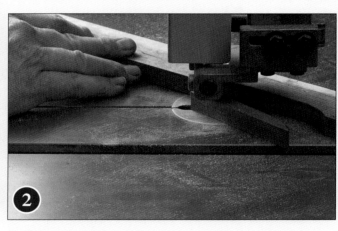

Cut the wood—Cut the wood to shape using a bandsaw, a scroll saw, or a coping saw.

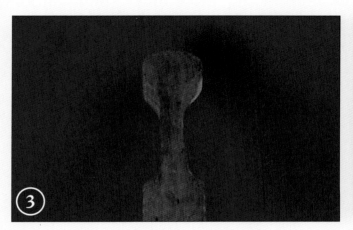

Finish shaping—Use the patternmaker's rasp to bring the stick to its finished shape.

Sand, stain, and add clear finish—Sand through 100 and 120 grits. If desired, add the stain of your choice to the walking stick. Once the stain has dried (if you used any) apply the clear finish of your choice.

BARK-ON STICKS
AND CANES

Leaving the bark on collected or bought sticks makes for interesting variations on the theme of walking sticks, canes, and staffs.

The first two bark-on projects shown here use a pine branch and a soft maple branch as primary materials. Both sticks were purchased on eBay. Searching eBay for such options allows more time for creating walking sticks and staffs in the shop and is especially helpful for those who don't live in places where it is permissible to cut small trees or where trees of any kind are available. This kind of project can readily be made in a city apartment since the only power tool necessary is a random orbit or finish sander. The third bark-on project is a sumac stick I harvested in the woods.

Begin by marking the length of the branch you wish to use (see Sizing Walking Sticks and Canes on page 25). Then, decide what tip you want to use and what handle.

The shiny hame ball makes a great handle on this pine branch cane.

PINE BRANCH CANE

For this first bark-on project, I used a pine branch that has some twists for interest and tight bark. By completing this project, you'll be learning some simple techniques for adding hardware to a natural cane. Just like the Flat Walking Stick in White Oak, this is a great beginning project because it uses simple techniques and requires very few power tools.

Start by drying the branch and using tung oil to seal it. Once the stick is dry and sealed, the bark should stay tight on this rustic walking stick. I think the shiny brass hame ball really dresses it up.

MATERIALS

- ◯ Pine branch, approximately 1¼" x 48", dried and sealed, cut to length
- ◯ 10', 12', or 16' measuring tape
- ◯ Random orbit sander, or finish sander, with 80- and 100-grit sandpaper
- ◯ Protective glove
- ◯ Cabinetmaker's rasp
- ◯ Patternmaker's rasp
- ◯ Finish of your choice (I used teak oil.)
- ◯ Rag for applying finish
- ◯ Brass hame ball
- ◯ Metal tip
- ◯ Screwdriver to fit brass screw
- ◯ Brass screw, #6 x 1" round head
- ◯ Epoxy

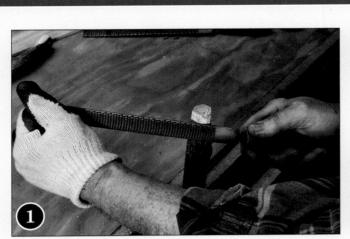

Shape the ends—My pine branch is getting a black metal tip and a brass hame handle. Start by power sanding the very rough bark on the pine branch using a random orbit sander. For shaping the ends, use a cabinetmaker's rasp for the rough work, and wear a glove to protect your fingertips.

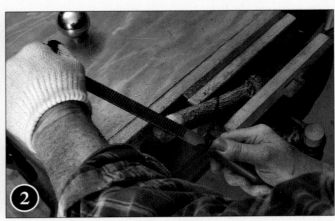

Rasp at an angle—To get a smoother finish as you approach the final shape, use the cabinetmaker's rasp at an angle to the surface. You may also switch to a patternmaker's rasp with its finer teeth.

Check the fit—Check the fit as you rasp. If you get it too small, you will have to cut off an inch and start over. That's not a big problem, but if you do it often, you'll end up with a mighty short walking stick. The closer you get to a finished size, the gentler you need to work.

Apply the oil finish—Fit the handle and the tip, but don't fasten either one. If all fits well, apply a very heavy coat of teak oil or polyurethane to the stick, except for the parts that actually fit under the tip and the handle. The teak oil dries rapidly: I got on four coats in one long day, applying each with a heavy hand (and a well-saturated rag).

Epoxy the handle—Once the finish dries so that you can handle the stick, mix just enough epoxy to coat the tip and handle surfaces well, and apply. Slide the ball top onto its epoxied area, and then drive a small brass screw through the standard hame ball hole.

Install the tip—Metal tips may be installed with a small brad through a hole in their bottom center, or they may be epoxied in place.

MAPLE STICK

Similar to the previous project, this maple stick is a rustic-looking branch to which I've added a top and a tip. A project like this one is a great opportunity to learn how to smooth out the bark while still keeping a natural look.

There are several options when it comes to leaving or removing the bark on a twisty stick like this. You can carve off the bark on the high areas and leave it on the low spots, or reverse that, taking off the bark on the low areas and leaving it on the high areas—or you can take it all off. For this stick, I chose to sand it all well, again using a random orbit sander, and let it be. I trimmed off a few shoot stubs on the band saw, which formed clear patterns down the shaft, along with the twist that the branch itself produced around the old vine. That left most of the bark intact, but quite smooth. Then, an oil finish completed the job.

The maple stick took a little less sanding than the pine, but did require digging out the vine that had given it its interesting pattern. Actually, there were some areas where the vine was so overgrown that I had to leave it in place.

MATERIALS

- ○ Maple branch, dried and sealed, cut to length
- ○ Random orbit sander, 80- and 100-grit sandpaper
- ○ Protective glove
- ○ Cabinetmaker's rasp
- ○ Patternmaker's rasp
- ○ Finish of your choice (I used a clear oil.)
- ○ Hame ball with apron
- ○ Tip of your choice (I used a brass tip.)
- ○ Epoxy

This maple stick got its twist from a deeply embedded vine, which I had to dig out of the bark.

Shape the shaft—Shape the handle end first, as shown, with a glove on the left hand to ease holding the cabinetmaker's rasp.

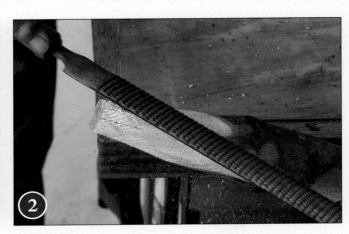

Rasp two ways—Rasping in two directions makes for a better job on this large a section.

Check the fit—As with other rasped parts, a size check is maintained as the sizing is done. In this case, an entire hame ball with apron is used, so that has to be slipped on in order to check sizing and to check where the apron is going to fall for epoxy placement. Make sure you check the fit of the tip and the handle often.

Slow it down—When the tip is close in size, switch to a patternmaker's rasp to slow the speed of final fitting.

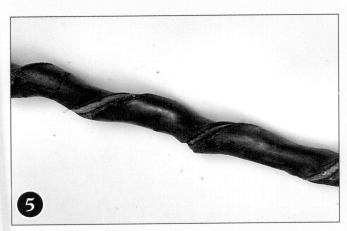

Sand and finish—Sand your stick to the desired smoothness, and then apply finish, making sure to leave top and end, where epoxy is to be used, clear of the finish. Clear oil does a great job of allowing the appearance of wood and bark to shine through. Application needs to be heavy and in several coats.

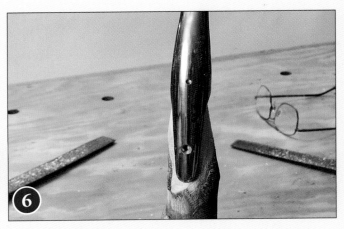

Install with epoxy—When both parts are a near perfect fit, or as close as you wish them to be, use epoxy to install them. Do not use an excess of epoxy. The stuff is a nuisance to remove even before it sets up, and is nearly impossible to remove afterward, at least without marring some of the work you've done. The tip actually has threads inside, so you can, if you wish, thread the tip end of the stick and work it on that way, making it easily replaceable (the tip used is heavy brass that takes a metal point or a rubber end, so it is unlikely to wear enough to need replacement for a very long time).

SUMAC STICK

The bend that makes the handle of this sumac cane is actually part of the root.

For the last bark-on project, we'll practice getting a high-gloss finish on a natural stick. The hardest part was finding the correct piece of wood. This piece is a chunk of sumac, with the bend at the handle actually being part of a root. These sticks are easy to find if you have access to woodland but require some work to get out (see Harvesting Roots, page 15). Allow the fresh stick to season indoors for at least three months, and then start working. Do not seal it before drying it.

The surface came down nicely—sumac sands and finishes well. I drilled the stick for a wrist thong—not yet added in the picture—and then applied five coats of high gloss polyurethane.

MATERIALS

- ○ Sumac stick, dried, cut to length
- ○ 10', 12', or 16' measuring tape
- ○ Holding device, such as the Workmate
- ○ Hand saw
- ○ Random orbit sander, 80-, 100-, and 120-grit sandpaper
- ○ Cabinetmaker's rasp
- ○ Patternmaker's rasp
- ○ Drill
- ○ High-gloss polyurethane
- ○ Rubber tip
- ○ Leather cording, for wrist thong

Hold the stick—This project had two snouts, but one was little more than ½" in diameter, so it was useful only as a way to hold the cane-in-waiting while the heavy rasping was being done.

Rasp the stick—Here you can see the heavy rasping getting started. There was a lot of crud and thick bark to clean off this stick, and I'm going to go for a very smooth finish so I'll use the random orbit sander once I'm done with the rasp.

Cut—Here I'm showing where to cut off the secondary root with a hand saw before continuing with rasping. Go from there to rasping all cut-off branches and any really rough spots. Once the rough rasping is done, step down to a finer grade of rasp and repeat the process; then, fetch the sander.

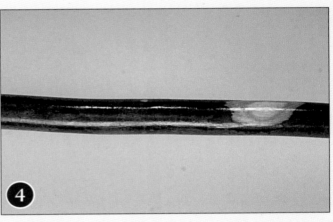

Sand and finish— Sand using 80 grit, and then move through 100 and to 120. Then, apply as many coats of high-gloss polyurethane as desired. I suggest at least three. Finally, add the tip.

WILLOW STICKS

Willow sticks with diamonds, or eyes, are readily available online. Some people make a lucrative hobby of searching the woods for the sticks. I found the ones I used for these two projects on eBay. You have to learn to bid wisely though, because they seem to be popular bits of material for many crafters and prices sometimes reach into the stratosphere for something you might also find locally, still attached to a tree root.

This willow stick is very handsome with its natural hoof-shaped handle.

WILLOW STICK WITH NATURAL HOOF HANDLE

This willow project will allow us to experiment making a natural-looking stick with the bark removed. Willow wood is particularly beautiful, so it is a great choice for this demonstration.

The willow stick I used is slender and light with several diamonds, or eyes, and has lots of bark stringers and rough spots on the surfaces. The hoof-shaped handle is a natural part of the stick.

The finished willow walking stick has a brass tip that had to be epoxied in place, though it struck me at the time that drilling a small hole in the bottom center of the brass cup would have let a screw be run up through the tip and into the end of the walking staff. The same procedure could be used on the sides so the screw wouldn't wear as rapidly.

MATERIALS

- ○ Willow wood, cut to length
- ○ Holding device, such as the Workmate
- ○ Drawknives, sizes of choice
- ○ Spokeshave
- ○ Dual-action random orbit sander, 80- and 100-grit sanding discs
- ○ Quarter-sheet finish sander and 100- and 120-grit paper
- ○ Finish of your choice (I used Minwax Wipe-On Poly.)
- ○ Disposable, or throwaway, brush
- ○ Rubber or metal tip
- ○ Small screwdriver
- ○ Screw, #4 x ¾" round head
- ○ Drill and twist bits sized to screw shank
- ○ Epoxy

Clean up with a drawknife—I started cleaning the shaft with a small carver's drawknife that is more easily controlled than a full-size drawknife.

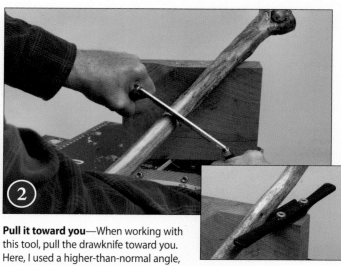

Pull it toward you—When working with this tool, pull the drawknife toward you. Here, I used a higher-than-normal angle, almost a scraping angle, because I wanted to remove mostly light shavings. It's also possible to use a spokeshave for this step.

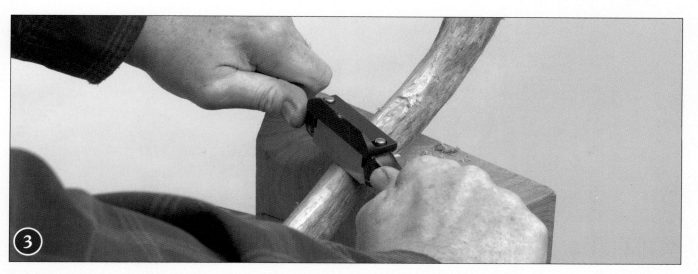

Push it away—Continue smoothing the shaft. In this situation, I found it easiest to push the spokeshave away from me. Other times, it will cut better on the pull stroke.

Sand the stick—After completing the heavier removals, move on to sanding. This dual-action random orbit sander is a real help in work like this. The finer orbit does a great job of finish sanding, while the harsher orbit removes stub ends and stubborn bits quite quickly.

Continue sanding—In addition to the dual orbits, the sander has a pad that is soft enough to ride into depressions and easily clean them up.

Use two hands—This is not a lightweight sander, so holding it as shown whenever possible, with both hands, is easier on the wrists and elbows.

Use the finish sander—Continue sanding up the shaft, but using a quarter-sheet finish sander, finally reaching the hoof end.

Sand the handle—Use the dual action sander's heavy removal mode to remove the sharp edges on the hoof-shaped upper end that is becoming the handle. Use your own hand to test the final shape.

Finish up—Get your finishing materials ready. I used Minwax Wipe-On Poly, but brushed it on in some areas and dipped it in other areas. Dipping was confined to the ends and limited to the distance that would fit in a quart can.

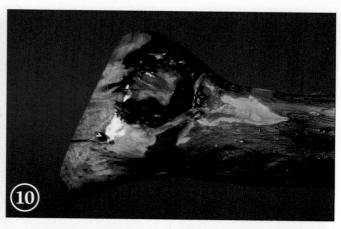

Dip three times—The hoof-shaped handle was dipped three times before the shaft was coated. Leave adequate drying time between coats so that sealing is completed with three dips.

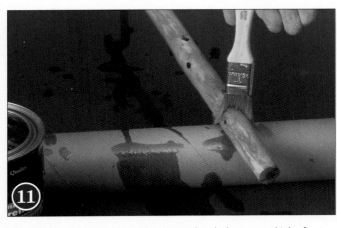

Brush it on—A disposable, or throwaway, brush does a good job of applying the polyurethane varnish. The bottom got several extra coats. This walking stick is intended for use with a rubber tip, so it doesn't need a surface cleaned for epoxy.

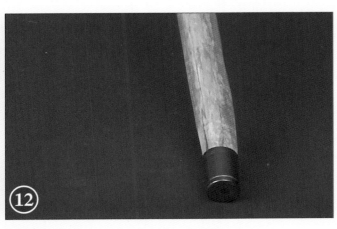

Install the tip—Once the finish has dried, install the tip.

USING DIAMOND WILLOW FOR YOUR STICKS, CANES, AND STAFFS

Willow with diamonds, often called "diamond willow," is very popular as a walking stick, cane, and staff material. Thought to form when the wood is attacked by fungus, the oval shapes that are created provide beauty and character that is especially appealing to many craftsmen. Many times the diamonds are even more prevalent than the ones shown on the sticks that I am using in the projects. More than just beautiful, willow is lightweight and carves well, increasing its value as a wood for many types of projects.

Photography by Gene Bremmer

These two walking sticks show great examples of very prominent diamonds.

Though they are partially hidden by the bark, the diamonds are still visible in willow trees in the forest.

This willow stick is light, useful, and attractive.
The brass ball makes a neat finish to the natural willow.

WILLOW STICK WITH BALL HANDLE

Just as with the Willow Stick with Natural Hoof Handle, this willow stick was created by removing the bark to show the beautiful wood and make a bark-off natural walking stick. Because this stick did not have a hoof-shaped handle, I added a brass hame ball.

MATERIALS

- ◯ Willow wood, cut to length
- ◯ Drawknife
- ◯ Random orbit or finish sander and paper in 80 and 100 grits
- ◯ Patternmaker's rasp
- ◯ Finish of your choice (I used Minwax.)
- ◯ Disposable, or throwaway, brush
- ◯ #0000 steel wool
- ◯ Mineral spirits
- ◯ Brass hame with apron
- ◯ Rubber tip
- ◯ Screwdriver to fit brass screws
- ◯ 3 small brass screws, #4 x ¾" round head
- ◯ Epoxy

Scrape it, then sand—The shaft was scraped reasonably clean, using the drawknife, and then sanded smooth.

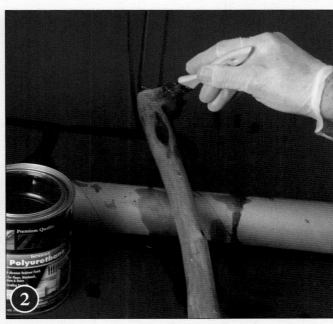

Brush polyurethane—Once sanded clean, the shaft was wiped with mineral spirits to remove dust and grease and allowed to dry. Then, polyurethane was applied with a brush. The bottom got an extra coat of finish because the rubber tip was being used.

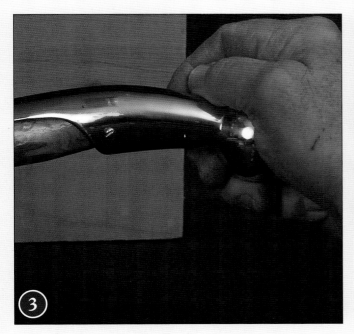

Fit the ball—Shape the top as needed with wood rasps and sanders to fit the hame handle, and keep a close check on fit as you go. The part that goes under the brass hame decoration needs a light coat of any clear finish to seal the wood. That is then cut with #0000 steel wool to provide a gripping surface for the epoxy. Slip the handle in place, and check the final fit. Remove, apply epoxy for the tongue and ball areas, and push the handle back onto the staff.

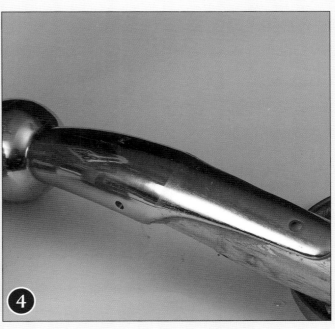

Use screws to finish up—To finish the job, drive three small brass screws into the holes on the hame handle to give it a finished look. They add very little to the strength of the bond to the handle, but the handle looks odd with empty holes. The screws might actually be used as fasteners, if you wanted to skip the epoxy. Also add the rubber tip.

PATTERNS FOR CARVED STICKS, CANES, AND STAFFS

Adding carved embellishments is a great way to add style to your walking stick, cane, or staff. In this section, you will find over 25 original patterns from renowned artist and author Lora S. Irish. Each design is presented from a variety of angles. The simple cane handles are presented in two side views, and the more detailed designs include up to four views. No matter what your style is, you're sure to find a design that will make a statement!

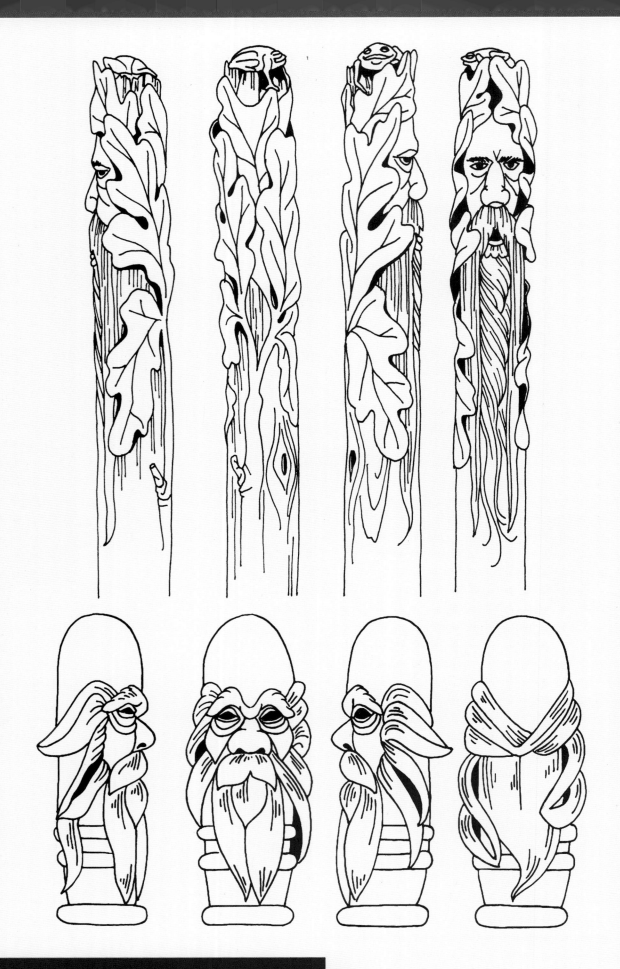

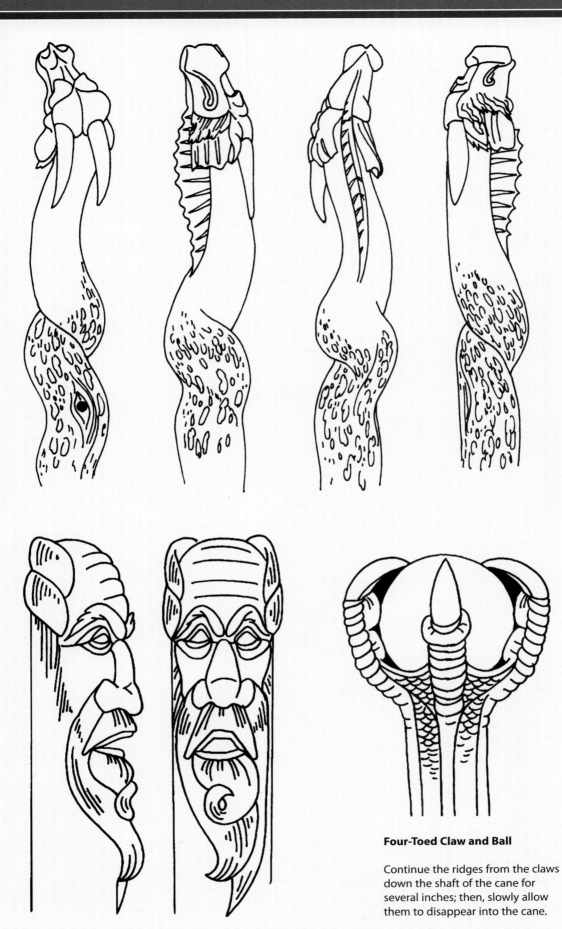

Four-Toed Claw and Ball

Continue the ridges from the claws down the shaft of the cane for several inches; then, slowly allow them to disappear into the cane.

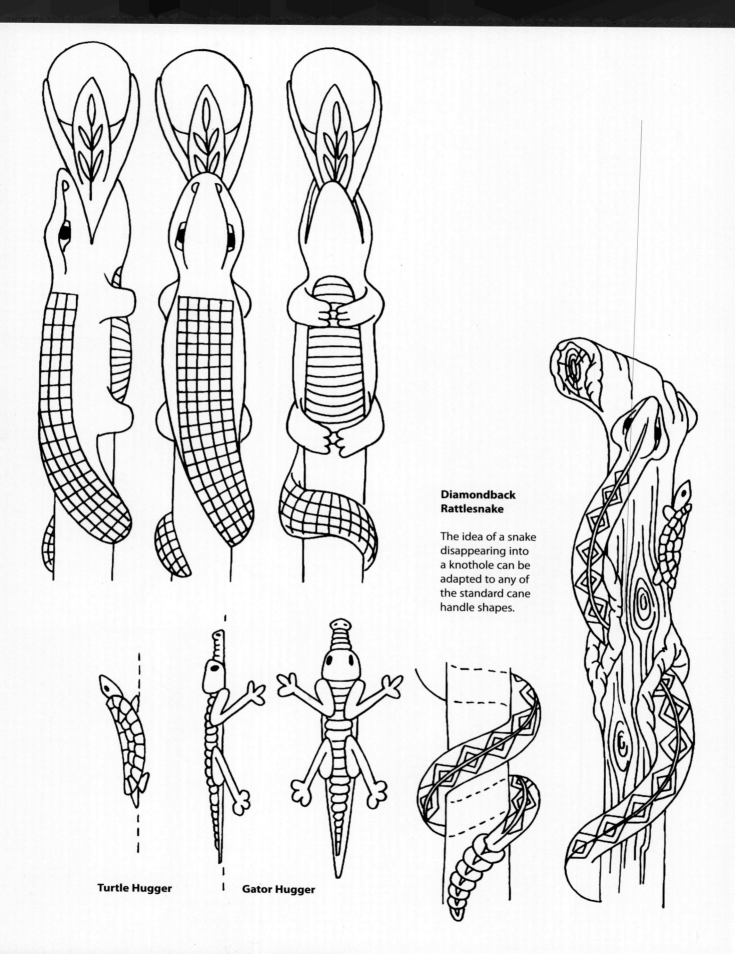

**Diamondback
Rattlesnake**

The idea of a snake
disappearing into
a knothole can be
adapted to any of
the standard cane
handle shapes.

Turtle Hugger   **Gator Hugger**

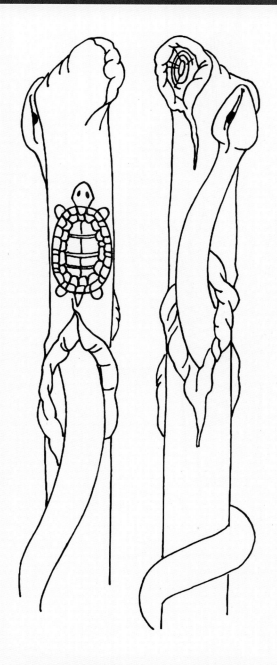

The rattlesnake has a triangle-shaped head that flares out away from the body area. The nose of the rattler is "sharp" compared with that of a nonpoisonous snake.

His skin texture is created with a fine-line checkering pattern. Try to avoid a fish-scale look on snakes.

Once the basic cane has been cut, establish where you want the knotholes. Place them on opposite sides of the stick. Next, add the snake body lines emerging from the knotholes.

Remember, this snake design will also work well with the snake going down the cane.

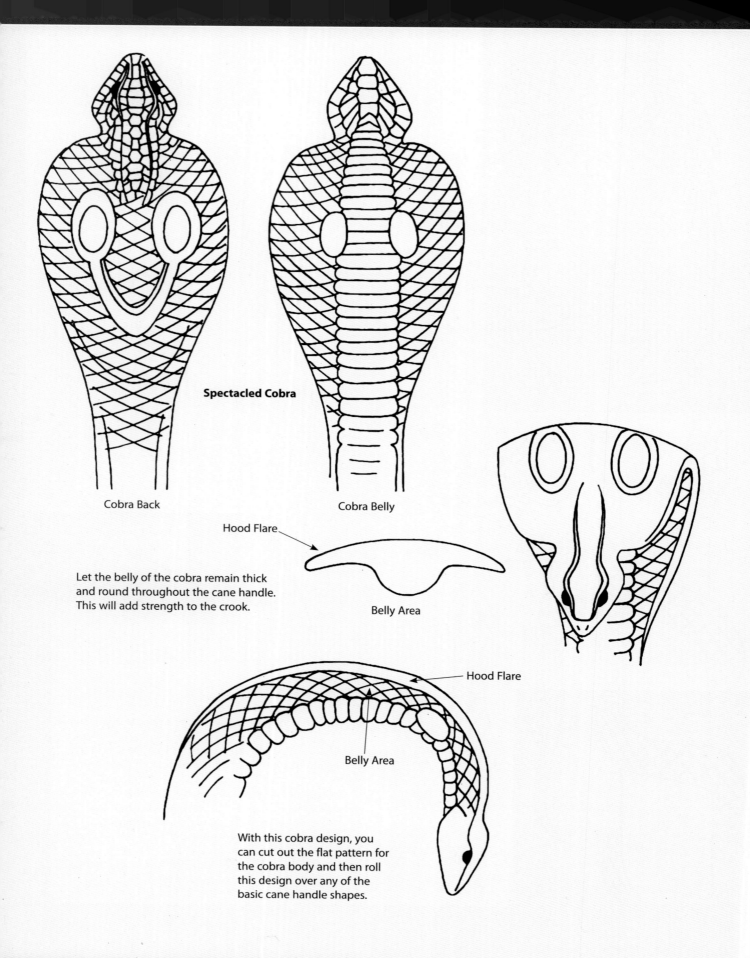

Spectacled Cobra

Cobra Back

Cobra Belly

Hood Flare

Let the belly of the cobra remain thick and round throughout the cane handle. This will add strength to the crook.

Belly Area

Hood Flare

Belly Area

With this cobra design, you can cut out the flat pattern for the cobra body and then roll this design over any of the basic cane handle shapes.

©Lora S. Irish

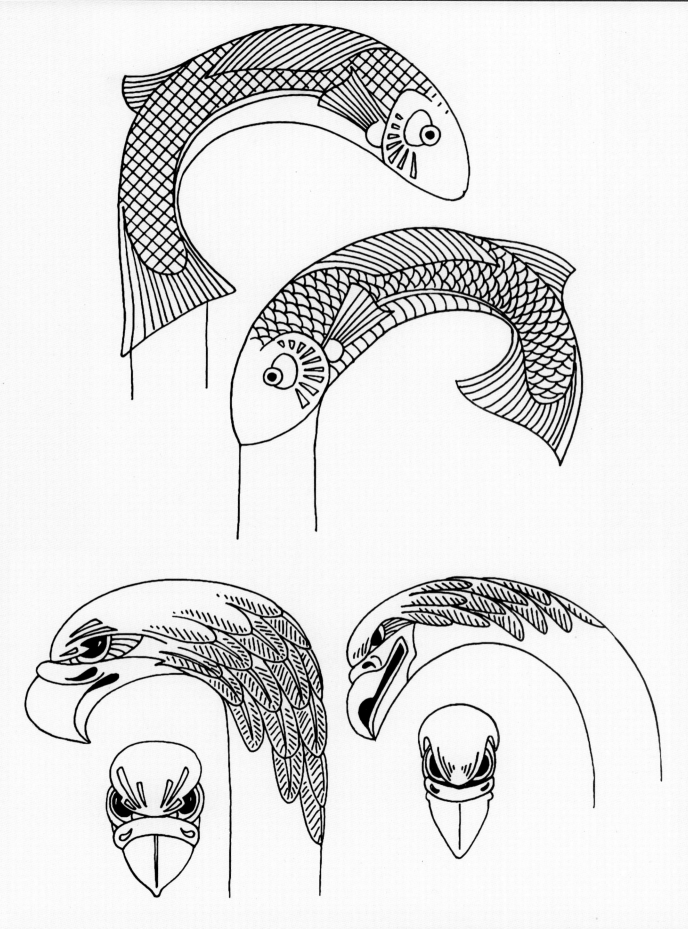

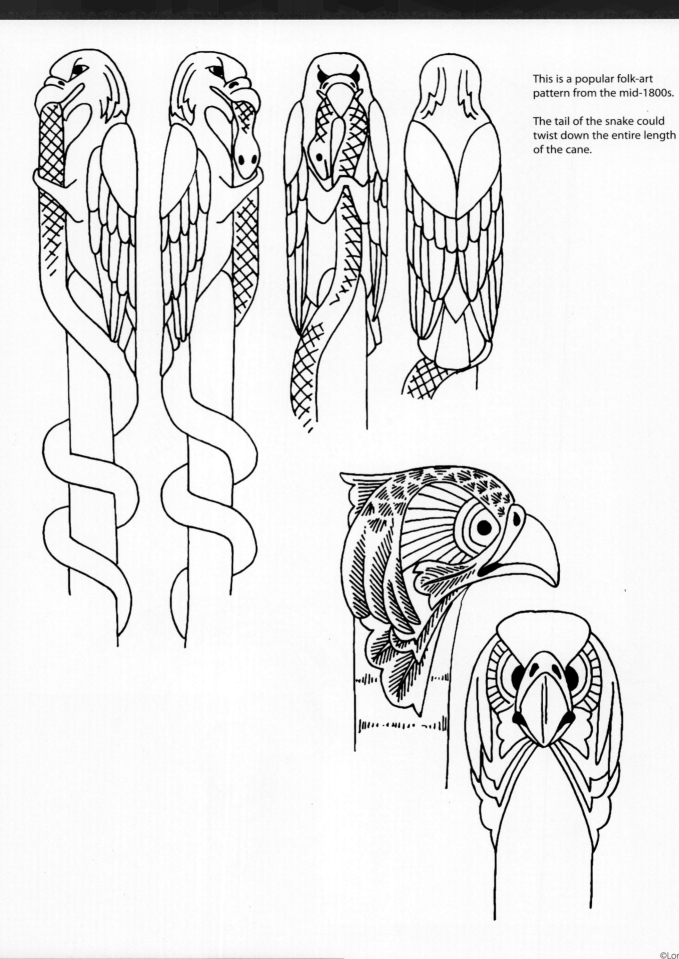

This is a popular folk-art pattern from the mid-1800s.

The tail of the snake could twist down the entire length of the cane.

©Lora S. Irish

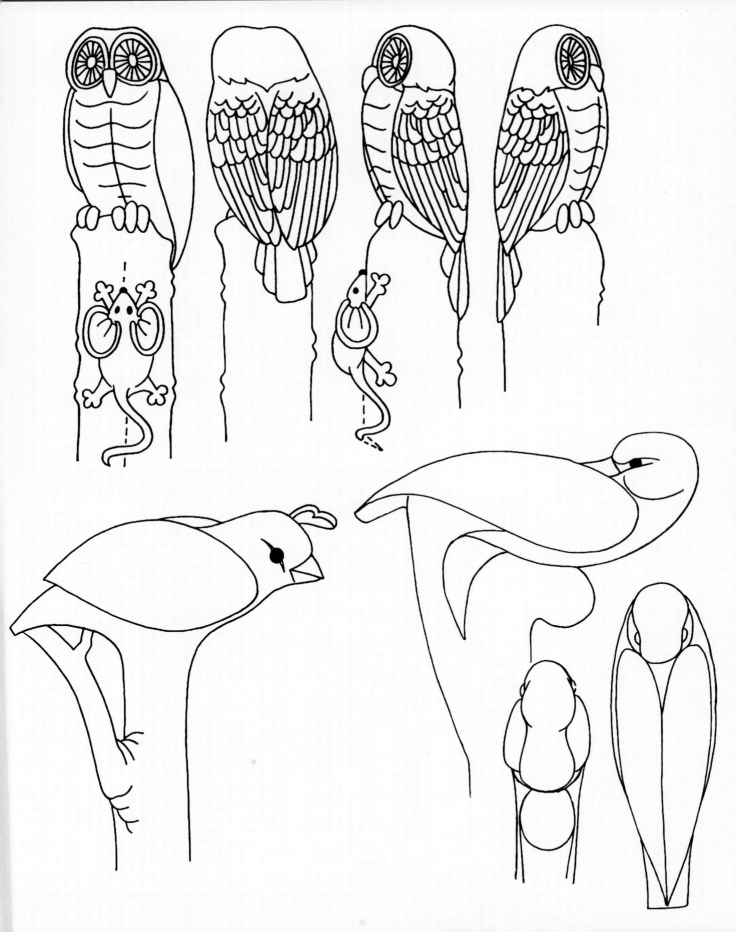

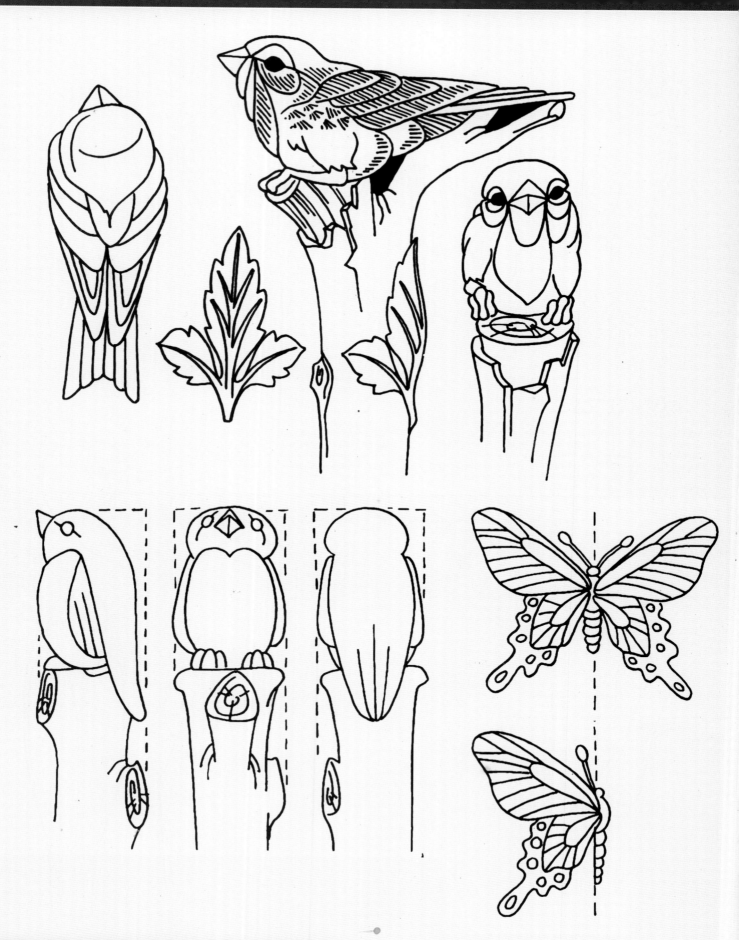

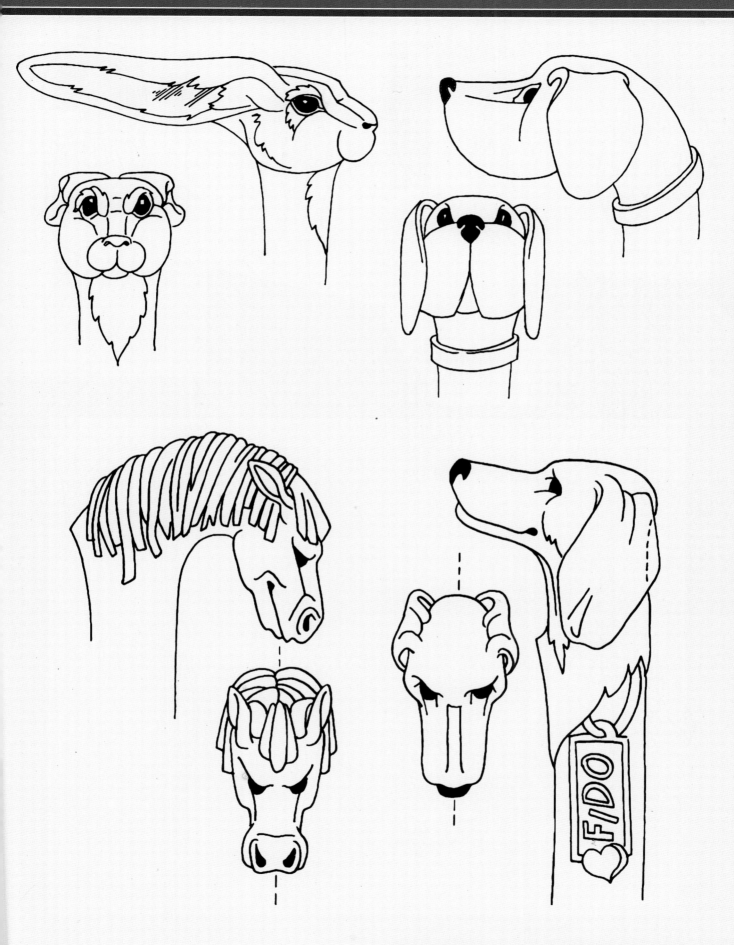

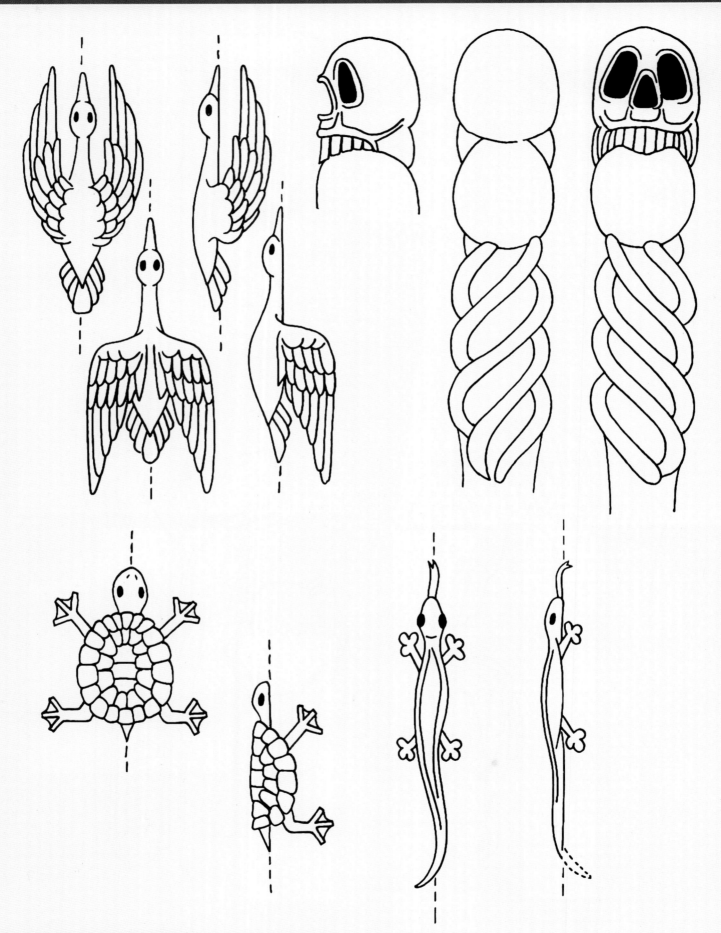

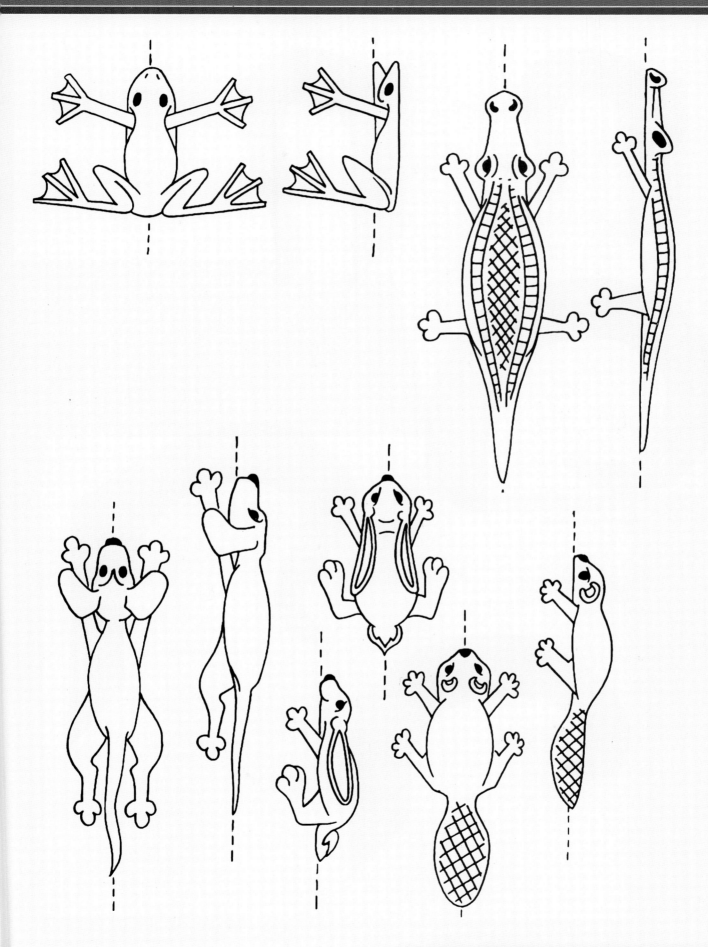

©Lora S. Irish

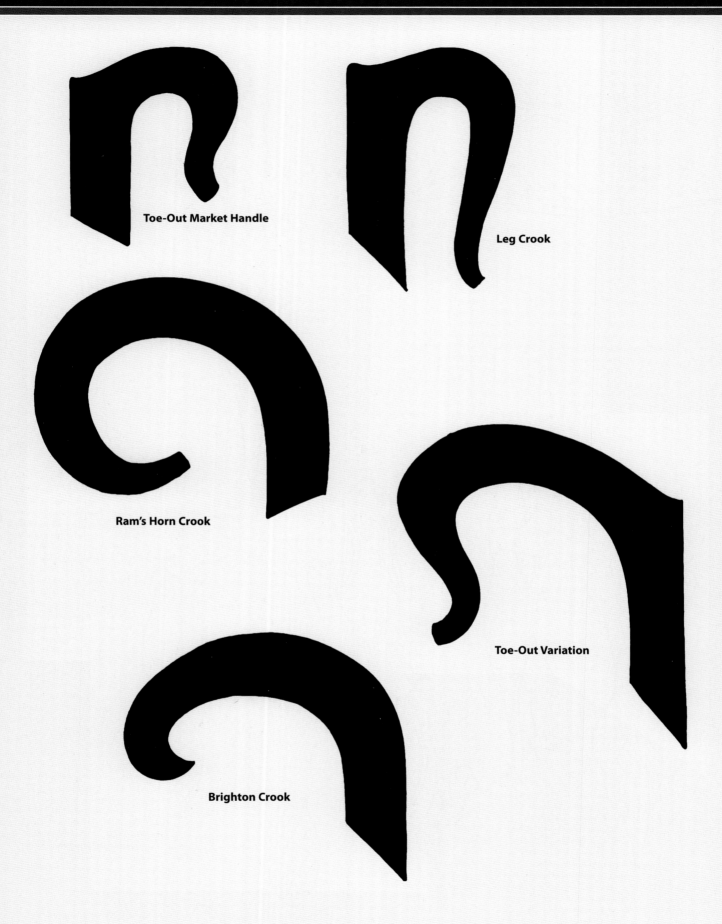

Toe-Out Market Handle

Leg Crook

Ram's Horn Crook

Toe-Out Variation

Brighton Crook

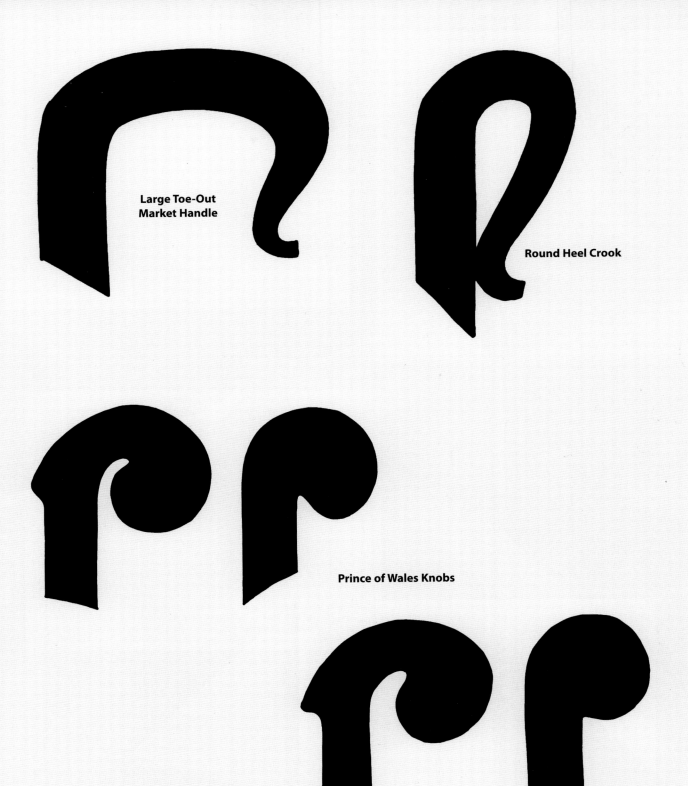

Large Toe-Out Market Handle

Round Heel Crook

Prince of Wales Knobs

TURNED
WALKING STICKS

Turning walking sticks on a lathe is a rewarding process. Actually, turning just about anything is a lot of fun, as artistic shapes develop very quickly. Turning may be the most readily creative woodworking skill any of us can apply, so the projects here are suggested as a start.

I used cherry for the canes in this section. Cherry is a fantastic wood to turn. It works with great ease and cuts without splintering or getting ragged, provided your tools are sharp. When you add its beauty and its ability to take a fine finish easily, cherry is hard to beat. Helping to make up my mind for using cherry on several projects was the fact that about six years ago I'd gotten a bargain on mill-run thick cherry, all of which was now ready to use.

Here's the walking staff in camera monopod mode, with the turned handle screwed off.

Here are all three parts of the turned cherry walking staff.

CHERRY WALKING STICK AND CAMERA STAND

This nifty turned cherry walking staff has a two-part shaft and a handle that threads off to expose a camera fitting so you can use it as a camera stand, or monopod.

This project has a lot going for it: It is useful as a walking staff; it serves as a camera monopod with a couple twists to remove the handle; and it is attractively made out of solid mill-run cherry. The only bad thing is that it takes a lot of time and some skill to build. You need to figure the length of the staff you want, as discussed on page 25. You need a lathe capable of handling at least 32"-long spindles and some skill at turning spindles. Other than that, the construction is straightforward, as is most stick making.

All of this cherry was gained from a single 6" wide by 12/4-thick board, about 4' long, which I happened on at a local sawmill. I started with the handle, using a cherry block about 11" long and 2½" square. That left plenty of room for changing handgrip designs as I went, but I really changed very little. The final handle is 9½" long and is fitted perfectly to my hand. The shafts are each 29" long, cut from 1¾" square cherry for the top and 1½" square cherry for the bottom.

Cherry is not obligatory. If you'd prefer, walnut is fine with this kind of light brass-colored trim, which also looks pretty good on hickory and oak. None of the hardware that touches wood is ferrous metal, so it won't create black stains in oaks.

MATERIALS

- Cherry block 11" long x 2½" square, for handle
- Cherry block 29" long x 1¾" square, for top
- Cherry block, 29" long x 1½" square, for bottom
- 6" combination square
- Stainless steel rule
- Carpenter's pencil
- Japanese pull saw
- Electric hand drill, Forstner bits (with center spur), and a ⅛" twist bit
- Lathe
- Turning gouge
- Skew chisel

- Small skew
- Mini cutting tool
- Sandpaper, 1"–2"-wide strips, cloth-backed (150, 220 grit)
- Finish of your choice (I used Liberon hard wax.)
- One two-piece threaded brass join
- Camera mount
- Decoration of your choice (I used a U.S. Marine Corps blazer button.)
- Double tip (accepts a rubber tip and a steel spike)
- Epoxy

Find the centers—I'm using a 6" combination square to find the centers on both ends of the turning blanks.

Mark the centers—Make the center-finder mark using a stainless steel rule. Do the other end the same way.

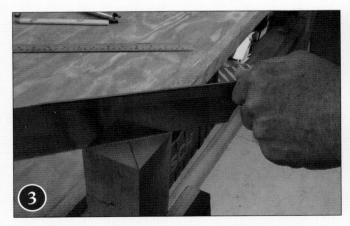

Saw the kerfs—I'm using a Japanese pull saw to cut the kerfs for the edges of the lathe spur to fit into. Over the long years, I've found pull saws work easiest when cutting kerfs in end grain.

Drill the center—Next up, drill a center hole where the kerfs cross. You don't need kerfs on the tail end, but drilling a hole can help.

Mount the center—Drive the live center into the end of the block, after making sure the spurs align with the kerfs.

Mount the block—Place the handle block in your lathe, get it tight and rotating cleanly, and then move the tool rest into place. Make sure the block edges don't strike the tool rest edge before you start the lathe. Also make sure you're as close as possible with that in mind, and that you can place your gouge correctly.

Turn the block—Knock the corners off the spinning block with the turning gouge; then, move in on the cylinder and remove all of the waste wood. Reset the tool rest so it remains close to the workpiece.

Smooth the shaft—Use a sharp skew chisel to smooth and size the cylinder.

Get a grip— Remember to turn off the lathe for this step! Use your hand to check the diameter of the handle. As the photo shows, the handle is still too fat for the hand it must fit.

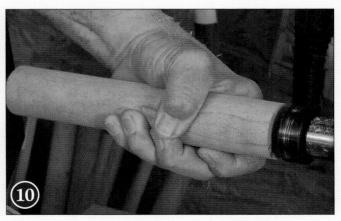

Keep on turning—Continue cutting down the handle until it fits comfortably. When it fits your hand, it's time to do the final patterning.

Mark the length—Mark one end of the turned handle for the bottom of the hand. Holding your hand in place, mark the other end of the handle for the top of the hand.

Lay out the grooves—The next step is to decide on groove placement on the handgrip area. I chose approximately 1" to the centers of each groove. Mark each increment, and then spin the handle by hand to make a mark all around the wood.

Make them dark—Turn on the lathe and gently press the pencil against the faint marks you see rotating. You may use any pencil for this marking, but I've found that using a power sander to sharpen a carpenter's pencil works best. Here, I'm using a scrap piece to demonstrate the technique.

Cut the grooves—Use a small skew to start the grooving. As you move along, cut second bevels for each groove, trying to keep them about the same sizes and angles as the first bevels.

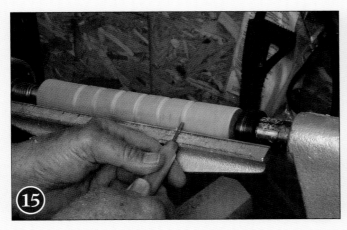

Try a mini tool—A mini cutting tool can help cut the grooves neatly and precisely, though a full-size tool rest, such as this, makes using mini tools difficult.

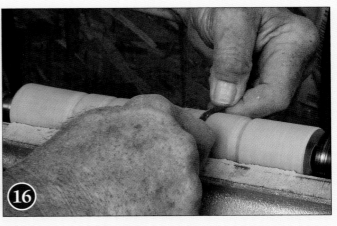

Sand the grooves—When the grooves are all cut, use a thin strip of 120- or 150-grit sandpaper to clean up the insides of the grooves. Norton makes some super sandpaper in narrow strips, 2" wide or so, that are cloth-backed and easy to tear into useful strips. You can also use pieces of a regular 1" cloth sanding belt.

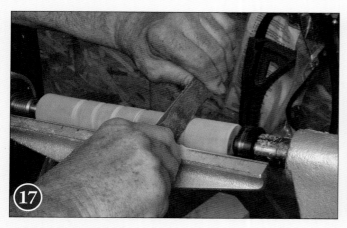

Sand the handle—Finish up the handle with cloth-backed sandpaper, at least 150 grit, with 220 grit preferable.

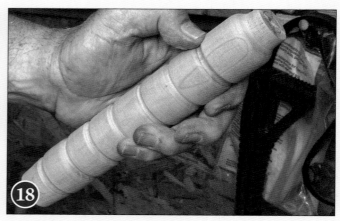

Wax the wood—I applied a Liberon hard wax finish while the handle was spinning at moderate speed on the lathe.

Turn the shafts—Make the same preparations—marking the centers, cutting the kerfs, drilling the holes—for the two longer spindles. Start with the thicker of the two pieces for the top, and turn the blank cylindrical on the lathe.

Continue turning—Continue shaping the shaft. Steady rests are a big help with long, thin spindles.

Sand and finish—Do finish smoothing of both spindles while they are on the lathe, using cloth-backed sanding strips. I also applied the Liberon wax finish at this point.

Install the brass joins—To fit the two-piece threaded joins, simply drill the top of the bottom section for one piece, and the bottom of the top section for the other piece. Epoxy in place and screw the two pieces together.

Install the camera mount—The camera-mounting screw thread that attaches the handle to the top of the shaft also comes in two parts. Drill to fit the coarse-threaded parts into the top of the shaft and the bottom of the handle. Make sure that you install the small threaded part sticking up from the top of the shaft; otherwise, you're going to have a stub handle instead of a monopod for your camera. Use epoxy again. Use the same mix of epoxy to install the tip to the lower shaft.

Measure the button—Before doing any drilling in the top of the handle, measure the decoration. I chose a blazer button with a U.S. Marine Corps emblem. Other services offer similar buttons, as do colleges, universities, and many other organizations. These decorations shouldn't be more than two-thirds the diameter of the top of the handle and should be of a durable material that won't react with the woods.

Fit the button—Drill a test hole and dry fit the decoration. It is hard to over-emphasize this point because if you blow the fit in the actual handle, then you have to turn another handle. Epoxy the button into the handle.

TWO-PIECE CHERRY CANE

Here is the two-piece cherry cane with both of its turned wood handles.

This two-piece cherry cane can be fitted with a brass handle, as shown here, or with either of the two turned wooden handles shown above.

This project is a two-piece shaft made to cane length or walking staff length (as discussed on page 25) and joined with brass inserts. For this project, I experimented with a choice of handles. I turned a ball and a ridged cylinder handgrip with a mushroom top, and I also tried out a cast-brass T-handle. These handles may be used on any cane in this book.

To make the two turned handles, I glued up a decorative billet more than long enough for both—it was 23¼" long x 2½" diameter after glue up. I started by ripping the cherry into two pieces, each about 2" x 4" x 2' long. Into that, I glued a 2"-wide piece of redheart, using Titebond III. When that had dried overnight, I ripped the resulting piece down its center again and glued in the piece of yellowheart. After another 24 hours, I planed the piece into a square billet. Length is only relevant if you're turning both objects on the same billet.

SIZING THE PROJECT

The mushroom-shaped handle is made for a walking staff or stick, which is most easily held slightly below chest height. The ball type fits easily on top of a cane or a walking stick or staff, regardless of height.

For this cherry walking stick, the top section is 22½" long, with a brass join at its bottom. It is about 1¼" in diameter at its widest point, with a slight bulge below the ¹⁄₁₆" diameter top that was sized to meet the bottom of the handles. The bottom tapers over its 23" length from 1" at the other half of the brass join down to ¾" where it is inserted into a white rubber tip.

The grips were laid out by holding the cylinder while it was on the lathe to get the appropriate spacing and size. This varies from person to person, so if you're doing one for yourself, measurement is very easy. If you're doing one for someone else, make sure you know how big that person's hand is. For more on sizing, see page 25.

MATERIALS

- 2 pieces of 2" x 25" cherry
- 1 piece of ¼" x 2" x 12" redheart
- 1 piece of ¼" x 2" x 12" yellowheart
- Wood glue (I used Titebond III because of a slim chance of wetness at some point in the project's life.)
- 1 hand clamp
- 6" combination square
- Stainless steel rule
- 10', 12', or 16' measuring tape
- Calipers
- Pencil
- Japanese pull saw
- Standard 10-tooth crosscut handsaw
- Electric corded or cordless drill with Forstner bits with a center spur and twist bits
- Lathe

- Skew chisel or scraper
- Parting tool
- Small gouge
- Regular turning gouge
- Large gouge
- Sandpaper, 220 grit
- Cloth-backed sandpaper
- Tung oil
- Wax (I used Renaissance.)
- Clear paste Minwax
- Wipe-on polyurethane
- Brass handle (optional)
- ¾" brass joins
- White rubber tip
- Epoxy

Glue up the handle blank—To make the two handles, glue up the yellowheart and the cherry; then, rip that in half and glue in a strip of redheart. Wood choice is up to you, but these are two easy-to-glue woods when also working with cherry. Then, mark and drill for the lathe centers as in the previous project (see page 111), and turn the glued-up billet into a clean cylinder, which is checked with a caliper set with a tape measure (see measurement specifics in the materials list).

Start with the ball—The ball is the more difficult of the two handles to turn. Begin by marking its length using a skew and turn the start of a neck between it and the rest of the billet using the gouge and the skew.

Reduce the neck—Continue to reduce the neck, separating the ball from the rest of the billet.

Form both ends of the ball—Use a skew chisel or a scraper, whichever tool suits your turning comfort level, and shape the end of the ball running down into the neck. Then, round off the other end of the ball toward the driving spindle using a small gouge.

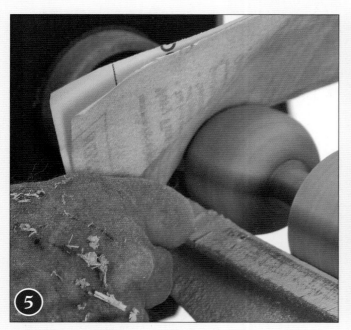

Complete the ball—Clean up and sand the ball, but don't make the neck too small yet. You are still going to turn the other handle on this same billet. Use strip sandpaper no rougher than 100 grit.

Turn the grip handle, mushroom top—After completing the ball, turn the mushroom-top handle using the gouge and the skew. The top is 2⅜" in diameter when finish sanded.

Form the grips—Use a regular turning gouge to reduce the size of the cylinder below the mushroom top and to form the grips. Stop often to make sure their diameter and spacing continue to fit your hand.

Complete the grip handle—A second knob at the bottom of the handle marks the end of the grip area and echoes the mushroom shape at the top. It is turned mostly with a gouge.

Make the flat end—Use a parting tool or a skew chisel to cut straight in at the bottom of the handle. The flat area here is necessary for a clean join with the cane shaft.

Sand and part them off—Sand the entire handle using folded pieces of sandpaper and strips of cloth-backed sandpaper. Start with 100 and continue through about 400 grit. Your turning should look like the inset before you part or saw the two handles off the billet. If you remove the turning from the lathe, use a pull saw to cut the excess free.

11

Drill holes in handles—Here are the two handles. The contrast among the three woods looks pretty good. Using internal calipers, measure the hole in the brass insert, and drill matching holes in the two handles.

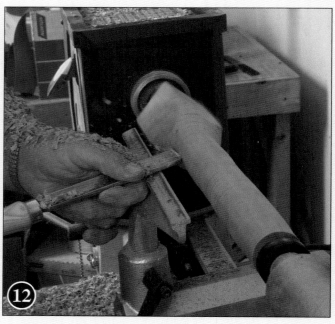

12

Make the shaft—For the shaft, use two 2" square billets. You can avoid whip problems by turning shorter spindles joined with brass inserts. Whip is the motion of the center of a slender turning that eventually turns into really bad vibration and makes accurate turning impossible. In the photo, I hadn't yet rigged up a lathe steady. Lathe steadies are attached to the lathe and have rollers placed at or near the center of the spindle being turned. The rollers touch the wood and prevent most whip problems. The top piece is 23" long, tapering from about 1¼" (back tapered to the handle's bottom) down to 1" at the brass join.

13

Reduce the diameter—Once you have turned the cylinder round with the large gouge and skew chisel, you'll have to remove a lot of wood to reach the finished size. Use the large gouge and skew chisel for this task also. Bring the head end of the billet down to size, and then work your way along.

14

Taper the bottom—The bottom, or second shaft, section has very little taper, from 1" at the join to about ⅞" where it enters the tip. Use a skew to turn a straight shoulder at the top, sized to fit the brass join.

15

Polish the wood—After you finish sand the shaft to at least 220 grit, shine up the wood by rubbing it with a handful of its own shavings while it spins on the lathe. This little trick imparts a beautiful luster to the cherry.

16

Turn the second shaft section—The second piece is the bottom of the cane shaft and is less thick, slimming from a maximum ¾" diameter to about a ½" diameter to fit inside the bottom cap.

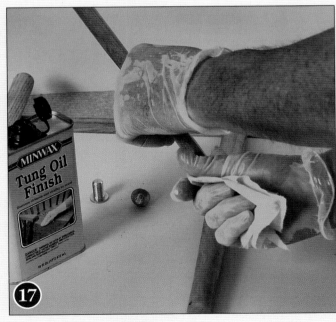

17

Place the joins and finish—This cane has ¾" brass joins. As in all cases with the threaded brass joins, ignore the threads, drill the holes barely snug, and then epoxy the joins in place. As with the first turned cherry staff, apply tung oil and let it dry; then, coat the shafts with wax. I started with Renaissance wax and added a couple final coats of paste Minwax in clear. Both the ball handle and the grip were given multiple coats of wipe-on polyurethane.

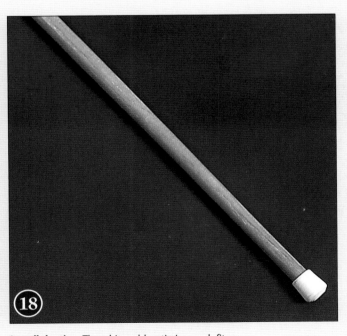

18

Install the tip—The white rubber tip is a push fit.

CHERRY- AND ROSEWOOD-HANDLED CANE

After turning the two cherry handles in the previous project (see page 116), I decided to make a third cherry cane with a T handle of cherry and rosewood. This handle is designed to accept a cane shaft drilled either into one end or into the side to provide a handgrip. It could be used on any of the cane shafts in the book.

I used epoxy to glue up the handle blank because of possible problems between rosewood and cherry with regular wood glues. Rosewood's oiliness and the included minerals in the wood make it difficult to glue to itself and even more difficult to glue to other woods. I glued the rosewood between two pieces of cherry. The rosewood was about ⅜" thick, while each piece of cherry was 1" thick. Both were 2⅜" wide. The cherry was from a batch I bought at a local sawmill and was green and rough. You may have to search wood dealers to locate rosewood.

The major discovery while turning the handle was the aroma of the rosewood. This wood is gorgeous, rare, and causes some people to have allergic reactions. It also smells a great deal like creosote, which, to me, is one of the less pleasant aromas around. Be warned that if you do use one of the rosewoods, you need some kind of dust mask while turning.

The one-piece cherry shaft is 1¹⁄₁₆" in diameter at the top before being doweled to fit the handle, and the tip is ⅞" to fit into a white rubber tip. The beading starts 11" up from the bottom and continues up with 1" center-to-center spacing of the nine beads. The overall length of the shaft is 34¼", giving the entire cane a length of 35¼", plus tip thickness.

The shaft and handle were both finished with satin polyurethane, with about six coats (and needing six more). The handle was epoxied to the shaft dowel before finishing.

A double-ended rosewood and cherry handle completes this beaded cherry wood cane shaft.

MATERIALS

- 1 piece of 1¾" x 1¾" x 38" cherry wood
- 1 piece of 1¾" x ½" x 10" rosewood
- 6" combination square
- Stainless steel rule
- Japanese pull saw
- Band saw (optional)
- Drill press table with ½"-diameter Forstner bits
- Electric corded or cordless drill with twist bits
- Lathe
- Large gouge
- Small gouge
- Skew chisel
- Small skew chisel
- Sandpaper, 100, 120, and finer grits
- Finish of your choice (I used satin polyurethane.)
- White rubber tip
- Epoxy

Mount the blank—Drill the handle blank for the lathe centers as usual (see page 111), and mount it on the lathe. In this photo, you can see that I used a bit too much epoxy in the joint—it actually dripped from the joint. Though it was costly and a bit sloppy, it didn't cause a problem during turning.

Turn cylindrical—Rough out the blank with a large gouge. The epoxy drools didn't seem to bother the turning tools.

Shape the handle—This handle is 8⅞" long and has one bullet-shaped end about 2" in diameter, a mushroom cap at the other end, and a gentle hand-friendly bulge in between. The smallest diameter, 1", is slightly behind the bullet head's shoulder. The center of the handle fattens up to about 1⅝" where the hole for the shaft is to be drilled.

Shape the ends—Use a skew chisel to form the curves at the end of the handle. Sand the handle before you remove it from the lathe to at least 120-grit smoothness. Smoother is better.

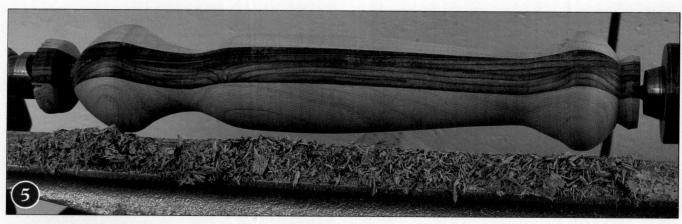

Complete the handle—The handle looks like this just before it comes off the lathe. If you're skilled with the skew, you can part off the waste. If not, take it to the band saw.

Drill the handle—Place the completed handle on the drill press table and drill to fit the shaft. I had necked the shaft down to ⅞", but ¾" is also fine. Use a flat-bottom Forstner bit and drill to the exact depth of the shaft dowel.

Turn the shaft—The shaft is a single length of cherry, no join. A series of decorative beads runs partway down the shaft, slightly closer to the thicker top end. The beads were cut with a small gouge and cleaned up with a small skew.

Turn the ends—Leave the shaft fat at both ends while working the center, and then turn the ends last. This maneuver reduces whip enough to make it possible to finish the project easily. Remember that you want to turn the shaft to fit the hole that you will drill in the handle.

Drill—Use the drill press to run a ½" Forstner bit into the handle. If you want to use a handheld drill with the Forstner bit, be sure that the bit has a center spur.

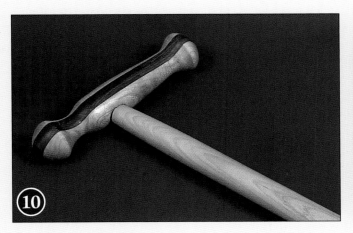

Coat with satin polyurethane—Use as many coats as you think the appearance demands.

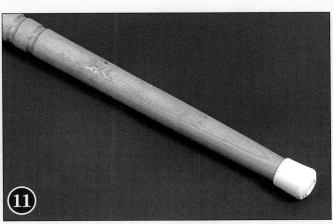

Install the rubber tip—The type I chose simply pushes onto the shaft.

Sassafras and Mesquite Two-Piece Cane

With this cane, I took two difficult-to-work woods in smaller pieces to make them easier to turn. Mesquite is so tough that a lot of cutting pressure is needed, even with sharp tools, and therefore it often breaks. Sassafras is less demanding but is prone to raggedness caused by whipping and vibrating. Neither is a desirable result. After learning the hard way—twice—that even with a steady rest, turning long, thin spindles (34"-plus long to under ¾" in diameter) wasn't a great idea, I went with a two-piece shaft: mesquite on the top and sassafras on the bottom. The mesquite section of the cane is somewhat shorter, so whipping is less of a problem, and you might get away without the lathe steady rest.

When the two woods were combined, decorative beading was made on the mesquite top section, and a tapering was done to the sassafras bottom section. This worked well, with the ever-present proviso that you take great care when drilling for the metal join parts so that the cane doesn't end up with a bend in its center. Though these two woods took quite a bit of work, the end result was well worth the time. Neither of these woods is readily available as found wood, so finding a mail order source, if you can't purchase the material locally, is a good idea.

The sassafras and mesquite cane comes apart at the brass join, so you can take it in a suitcase or briefcase. The brass handle looks really good against the lustrous mesquite.

MATERIALS

- ○ 1 piece of 2" x 2" x 20" mesquite wood
- ○ 1 piece of 2" x 2" x 20" sassafras wood
- ○ Calipers
- ○ 10', 12', or 16' measuring tape
- ○ Carpenter's pencil
- ○ Lathe
- ○ Skew chisel
- ○ Parting tool

- ○ Narrow skew or square-end chisel
- ○ Sandpaper to 400 grit
- ○ Teak oil
- ○ Rag
- ○ Eagle head handle (Veritas from Lee Valley)
- ○ Brass join fitting
- ○ White rubber tip

Rough turn the mesquite—Start with a mesquite billet for the top section of the cane, about half the full length of the cane, turning it quickly with a skew to its finished ¾" diameter. Mesquite is a hard wood to turn simply because it is a very hard wood. A length of 20" or less makes it a lot easier to turn.

Measure the join—Use a caliper to measure the brass fitting that will join the two parts of the cane. You want to match the end diameter of the wood to it.

Turn the join end—The parting tool, checked by a caliper, quickly brings the join end of the mesquite down to the size that matches the brass fitting.

Lay out the beads—Make beading marks about 1" apart for ¼"-wide decorative beading. Use a measuring tape or steel rule and mark them with a pencil.

Darken the marks—Use a very sharp carpenter's pencil to run the marks all the way around the cylinder.

Cut the waste—Use a narrow skew or a square-end chisel to reduce the waste wood in between what will become the decorative beads.

Reduce the diameter—Continue removing waste wood from between the future beads until these spaces all reach the same depth.

Round the beads—Use the skew chisel to round over the beads, but don't undercut them.

Sand the mesquite—The mesquite is very hard and takes a beautiful polish, but you have to sand it through 400-grit paper.

Get ready to finish—Here are the sassafras (see Sassafras Cane with One-Piece Shaft on page 130 for turning instructions) and mesquite cane parts, with the join installed and the handle and tip alongside, ready for finish. The bottom, or sassafras, part is longer and needs more sanding because of the way the wood roughs up.

Wipe it on—Apply the finish with a soft rag, such as an old T-shirt. The finish is teak oil, which is easy to apply, dries reasonably quickly, and can be easily recoated, or may be overcoated with almost any other finish. By itself, it gives the wood a soft luster without a thick build-up.

Install the hardware—Once the finish has dried, install the joins, the tip, and the handle.

SASSAFRAS CANE WITH ONE-PIECE SHAFT

The Sassafras Cane with One-Piece Shaft is one of the few long one-piece sticks in this book because of the level of difficulty in cutting a 36"-long piece of wood on a lathe once it is down to a near-useful diameter. Even with a shopmade whip-reducing lathe steady rest, problems can still arise. However, I was able to create this nice sassafras cane with an elegant handle and an interchangeable tip.

MATERIALS

- ○ 1 piece of 2" x 2" x 36" sassafras wood
- ○ 6" combination square
- ○ Stainless steel rule
- ○ Calipers
- ○ Carpenter's pencil
- ○ Japanese pull saw
- ○ Soft-faced hammer
- ○ Electric drill with ⅛" twist bit
- ○ Lathe
- ○ Large gouge
- ○ Skew chisel
- ○ Small gouge
- ○ Sandpaper, 100 and 220 grit
- ○ Finish (I used Minwax paste wax.)
- ○ Rag
- ○ Double tip

This light-colored sassafras cane has an elegant brass handle. The handle has a ¾" threaded socket, but the parts were connected with epoxy.

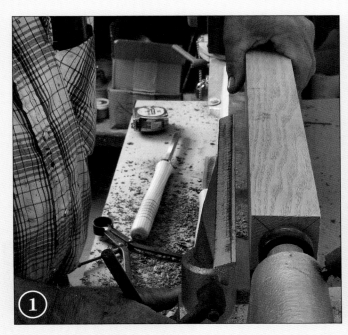

Set up the turning blank—Start with the standard procedure of marking the center of the billet, cutting saw kerfs for the driving spurs using the pull saw, and drilling for the spur center, using an electric drill and a ⅛" twist bit (see page 111). This billet was 2" square.

Mount the billet—Install the billet in the lathe carefully, making sure it is centered and held tightly.

Turn the cylinder—A large gouge removes lots of wood, making the chips fly. The chips can really fly as the square billet comes down to a cylindrical shape.

Caliper the diameter—As you bring the cylinder down to size, check the diameter with a caliper. To clean up the rough fibers, and for lighter cuts, use a skew chisel.

(5)

Use a steady rest—The sassafras is bendy, and the shaft vibrated and whipped no matter how light a cut was taken. So I brought in a homemade steady rest. It's just a plywood bracket with some old roller skate wheels on slotted mounts so they can be brought into contact with the turning.

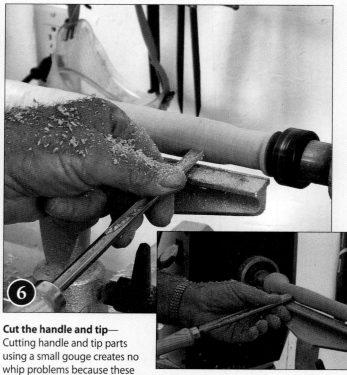

(6)

Cut the handle and tip—Cutting handle and tip parts using a small gouge creates no whip problems because these short areas are well supported by the lathe head and tail pieces.

(7)

Smooth the shaft—As the skew chisel moved toward the center of the shaft, the whip became severe, and the steady rest came into play. The whipping action was readily visible both in the motion and in the results, a sort of wavy spiral on the slender shaft.

(8)

Check the diameters—Carefully caliper the cylinder diameters at the ends and in the middle to make sure they fit the intended tip and handle. Use the skew to make the tip just enough oversize to need the attention of a soft-faced hammer to drive the shaft into the tip, while the top is left slightly less oversize to allow screwing the handle in place without epoxy. However, if you prefer, either may be cut to an easy push fit and the holes lined with epoxy.

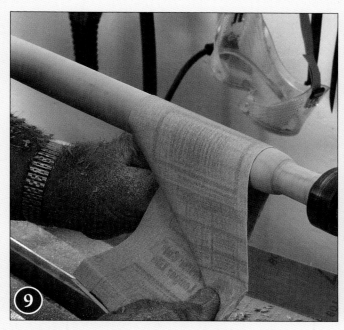

(9) Sand the shaft—The shaft is left a bit fat, so shaping the handle and tip ends is needed to get a good fit with the brass parts used. To shape, sand with the spindle spinning on the lathe. Keep the speed up and use a half-width of sandpaper in 100 grit or finer.

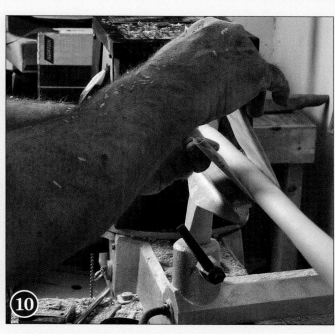

(10) Try back sanding—You can even leave the rest in place because you can back sand, which is nothing more than sanding behind the work as the photo shows. The paper used, from start to finish, was Norton's 3X 220 grit. It takes rough material off very quickly, yet gives a superlatively smooth finish. It also lasts a long time.

(11) Finish with wax—The only finish on this cane is a couple of coats of Minwax paste wax.

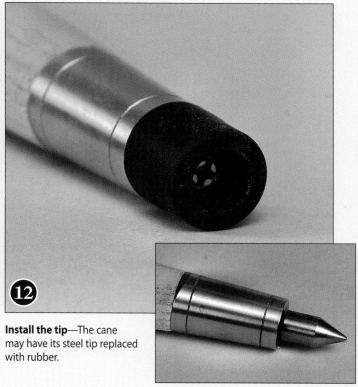

(12) Install the tip—The cane may have its steel tip replaced with rubber.

LAMINATED CANES

Laminated canes can be the most variable of the huge selection of canes available because each ply can be a different wood, a different color, and a different thickness. Overall, lamination is a great deal easier to do than any other form of wood bending that works for canes. Start with the form, cut the wood into plies on the table saw or band saw, and begin with as many plies as you can handle at one time.

This crooked-handle cane consists of a dozen thin layers of wood, alternating oak and cherry, glued together around a form.

LAMINATED CHERRY AND OAK CANE

One way to make the crook for a cane handle is to laminate thin pieces of wood together and bend them around a form. This cane uses alternating layers of cherry and oak, starting at the inside with one cherry strip, going to two oak next, and finally ending with four strips of cherry. You may wish to do it entirely differently, or with different woods, but check bendability before starting. To check bendability, simply cut a ply or two to the thickness you plan to use. Then, bend it around the jig. If it cracks, it needs to be thinner, or another wood needs to be used.

MATERIALS

Laminations:

- ○ 1" x 6" x 38-40" oak and cherry blanks
- ○ Table saw or band saw
- ○ Push stick
- ○ Eye protection
- ○ Glue, such as Titebond II
- ○ Clamps
- ○ Jig
- ○ Disposable paintbrush or trim roller
- ○ Clamping block or caul
- ○ Apron pocket plane
- ○ Cabinetmaker's rasp
- ○ Tip
- ○ Sandpaper, through 200 grit
- ○ Polyurethane (I used Minwax Wipe-On Poly.)
- ○ Rag

MAKING THE BENDING JIG

The jig is probably the hardest part of the project. It consists of a bending form fastened onto a particleboard base with pegs in holes to help trap the laminations while you festoon them with clamps.

I cut my bending form from a chunk of 2 x 8 that was on hand, using a 6" radius for the top. I suggest you use a slightly smaller radius: This one is not quite perfect for my hand, though it fits larger hands well (see page 25 for more information on sizing). A 5½" radius might be ideal.

MATERIALS

Jig:

- ○ Chunk of wood, like 2 x 8; must be as long as finished cane
- ○ 12" wide particleboard
- ○ 1" dowels
- ○ Band saw
- ○ 1¼" x #8 square drive screws
- ○ Handheld drill or drill press and 1" flat-bottomed Forstner bit
- ○ Shellac
- ○ Polyurethane
- ○ Paste wax

1. Cut the jig using a miter saw so its total length is 34"; cut away square on the straight section beyond the crook so the clamps fit easily. Use a bandsaw for the curved cuts. Use 1¼" x #8 square drive screws, spaced about 6" apart lengthwise and 2" to 3" across the narrow parts, to attach the 12"-wide particleboard base to the bending form.

Use a flat-bottomed Forstner bit (with a center spur if you are using a handheld drill and without a center spur if you are using a drill press) to drill 1" holes for the pegs in the base about two-thirds the thickness of the particleboard. I drilled nine holes, spaced as I thought necessary, leaving 1½" between the inside of the dowel pegs and the jig surface.

2. Cut the 1" dowels to 2½" long and coat them with shellac. Put a clear coat of polyurethane on the top parts of the jig, followed by paste wax on all the surfaces likely to be touched with glue. Paste wax on the jig surfaces will help them resist drooling glue.

3. Set up the jig and get out all the clamps you will need before you apply glue to the thin strips of wood.

MAKING THE LAMINATIONS

Now we're ready to make the laminations that will compose our cane. To avoid the problems and dangers of ripping thin pieces between the fence and the blade, reset the saw's rip fence for each cut. That way, the bulk of the workpiece is between the blade and the fence, and the falling board—the thin strip you want—is always to the outside of the blade. Use the saw guard with its riving knife to achieve this. Take the usual precautions: Use a push stick, wear eye protection, and do not stand in the path of the workpiece or the ripping. Unless you use a system of spacer blocks, resetting the fence for each cut means your laminates won't be exactly the same thickness, but that doesn't really matter. Pretty close is close enough.

Keep these things in mind as you are working. First, the thinner you cut the strips, the more you need; however, this means that you can make tighter and more complex curves. A ¹⁄₁₆" strip of white oak or cherry bends easily. I made my strips ³⁄₃₂" thick, which worked on my jig. At ³⁄₃₂" thick, 11 strips make a 1"-diameter cane. At ¹⁄₁₆", you would need 16 pieces.

Second, expect to get fewer strips than you might at first hope because the table saw kerf is greater than the strip thickness. (The kerf is the thickness of the cut made by the saw blade.) A blade with a thin kerf reduces the loss to about the same width as the strip itself. With a regular blade, a ³⁄₃₂" strip will consume approximately ¼" off the workpiece, and 11 of them will consume almost 3" of width. Cut at least six extra strips for those times when you snap or otherwise mess up a strip.

Prepare the oak and cherry blanks, 38" to 40" long by 1" thick and at least 6" wide, for the laminations. Cut the strips on a table saw with a zero-clearance insert using a substantial pushstick. A bandsaw may also be used.

You want to end up with laminations that are uniformly thick and just thin enough to bend around the curve you've chosen. This strip is too thin. It's simplest to make them to the final size on the table saw since the thickness planer is liable to just chew them up. If you don't already have a zero-clearance plate for your table saw, make one (see sidebar below).

MAKE A ZERO-CLEARANCE THROAT PLATE

Use the table saw's standard throat plate for a template and cut the zero-clearance plate, using a piloted (pattern) bit on a router. You can use plywood, medium-density fiberboard, or a soft aluminum alloy for the insert. Another method is to use a scroll saw or a band saw to cut the curved shape and smooth it with sandpaper. The resulting plate must be a tight push fit in the throat of the saw.

Mark your table saw fence at 1¼" above the plate surface, after lowering the blade all the way. Make sure the prospective zero-clearance plate is held tight, either with the fence and a block clamped to that or with clamps at each end of the table holding a board down over the plate. Slowly raise the turning blade into the plate until you can see the teeth reaching the mark on the fence. This will be your maximum depth of cut for the slender lamination pieces.

Use a cut-off finishing nail to make a pin for the plate (most plates have a locating pin on one end: Make sure you get it in the right end, in the right place, using the standard plate as a pattern) so that it remains centered. If your saw requires screws to hold the plate in place, drill and countersink holes for those.

One note: On some table saws, a full-size 10" blade cannot be lowered far enough to accept the blank for the zero-clearance plate. If that's the case, use one outside blade from an 8" dado set or any 7¼" or 8¼" circular saw blade, to start the cut. Always finish penetrating the plate with the 10" blade you'll be using for your cuts. A 30- or 40-tooth finish ripping blade (flat top grind) is best.

Gluing up

For these steps of the process, it's important to choose a glue that is water resistant. Water resistant properties are important for this project because some of the laminations would release enough moisture to weaken standard wood glues.

Once you've cut the strips, lay them out in order and select the glue you want to use. I used Titebond II because it's reasonably easy to clean up and is highly water resistant without being waterproof (which always means harder to clean up). Here's a mixed batch of oak and cherry strips ready to be glued.

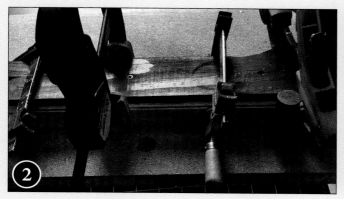

Clear a space for the jig. I set mine off the workbench and used the workbench edge to glue the strips, working four strips at a time because of the relatively short open time of the glue I'm using. Four strips at a time basically means three glue-ups, unless you're very speedy. Use a disposable paintbrush or a disposable trim roller to spread the glue. Spread the strips so they are tight together. Because my top curve wouldn't close properly, I had to add a band clamp to the mix. I clamped right over the band clamp once that was in place, making sure (as much as possible) that all edges were aligned and straight.

Clamp every 4" to 6"; 4" apart is better. You'll also get better results if you use a clamping block, or caul, on the outside of the curve. That's easy on the straight sections, but you'll have to calculate its shape pretty close for the curved handle, and you might need to make the caul in several sections. A caul is a block formed to the exact shape of the jig; it has a flat back so that clamps can press without slipping and the shape being clamped is correct. Let the set-up dry for 24 hours. When the clamps finally come off, you should have no delamination.

CLEANING UP

Once the laminations are glued up and have dried completely, we're ready to put the finishing touches on our cane. The majority of the work will be making the laminations smooth, and then we'll finish the can and add the tip.

Use a small block plane to level the laminations and begin to form the round cross section after taking the cane out of the jig.

Shape the edges with the plane and with a rasp, depending on location, and then sand everything smooth.

Use the rasp to reduce the end that accepts the rubber tip.

The tip should be a snug press fit. These are chair leg tips, and you can buy them at the hardware store in cards of four for under three bucks, or you can spend about four bucks each for something similar in a pharmacy. The pharmacy ones are heavier though.

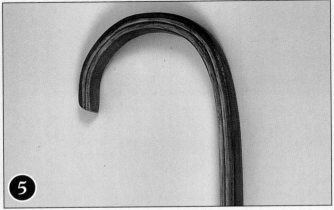

Sand the cane to 200 grit, wipe it with mineral spirits, and apply four coats of Minwax Wipe-On Poly.

INDEX

RESOURCES

Domestic and Exotic Hardwood Lumber:
Gilmer Wood Company
2211 NW St. Helens Road
Portland, OR 97210
(503) 274-1271
www.gilmerwood.com
ann@gilmerwood.com

Exotic Woods and Exotic Wood Segmented/Laminated Bowls:
Hobbit House Inc.
Paul Hinds
www.hobbithouseinc.com/personal/woodpics
wwodpics@hobbithouseinc.com

General Hardware:
McFeely's
PO Box 44976
Madison, WI 53744
(800) 443-7937
www.mcfeelys.com

Hames and Hardware:
Woodworker's Supply Inc.
1108 North Glenn Road
Casper, WY 82601
(800) 546-9292
www.woodworker.com

Handles and General Cane Hardware:
Lee Valley Tools Ltd.
PO Box 1780
Ogdensburg, NY 13669
From USA: (800) 871-8158
From Canada: (800) 267-8767
From other countries: (613) 596-0350
www.leevalley.com
customerservice@leevalley.com

Mesquite:
Thunderbird Hardwoods
On the Square in Llano, TX 78643
(830) 798-5533
www.tbird-hardwoods.com
sales@tbird-hardwoods.com

Sassafras:
Hazelton Woodworks
Route 3 Box 148
Bruceton Mills, WV 26525
(304) 379-8612
www.hazwoodworks.com

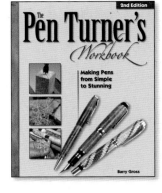

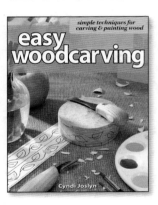